About the Author

I am a family man with a grown up son and daughter who are thirty-five and forty-two now, and a credit to their amazing mum, Leslie, who is the inspiration for this book of amazing memoirs. Through all my years, my passengers would all say to me that I should write a book when I retire! So I did! This is my first book and I have really enjoyed the experience of writing down all my great stories and actually getting it published so that everybody will get a chance to read all about my life as a taxi driver.

CONFESSIONS OF A TAXI DRIVER

Adrian Durtnall
___

CONFESSIONS OF A TAXI DRIVER

Vanguard Press

VANGUARD PAPERBACK

© Copyright 2024
Adrian Durtnall

The right of Adrian Durtnall to be identified as author of
this work has been asserted by him in accordance with the
Copyright, Designs and Patents Act 1988.

All Rights Reserved

No reproduction, copy or transmission of this publication
may be made without written permission.
No paragraph of this publication may be reproduced,
copied or transmitted save with the written permission of the
publisher, or in accordance with the provisions
of the Copyright Act 1956 (as amended).

Any person who commits any unauthorised act in relation to this
publication may be liable to criminal prosecution and civil claims for
damages.

A CIP catalogue record for this title is available from the British
Library.

ISBN 978-1-83794-215-2

Vanguard Press is an imprint of
Pegasus Elliot Mackenzie Publishers Ltd.
www.pegasuspublishers.com

First Published in 2024

Vanguard Press
Sheraton House Castle Park
Cambridge England

Printed & Bound in Great Britain

Firstly I wish to say how proud I am of my son and daughter, Russell and Aimee. Leslie and I gave them both fantastic childhoods full of fun and adventure! They have both grown into independent, successful adults! My dear mum, Eve, and my late dad, Ken, have been brilliant supportive parents to my sister Sue and I throughout our whole lives, and we will be forever grateful! In my early years of marriage when my sister was single she would always lovingly say how she envied the happy, loving and beautiful relationship we had with each other! Well now Sue's wishes have come true and she too has her own loving family with Tom and her daughter Emily! Our lifelong friends, Wendy, Andy and Lorna have been there for us through thick and thin and especially all the holidays, parties and many fun times. They all loved Leslie and were true and loyal friends who took her on many shopping trips while I was at work. After ten years working outside Asda I made many friends with all the regular shoppers, staff and management, plus the drivers, Alf, Colin, Will, Derek, Justin, John, Chris, Alan and Pete. Other taxi drivers over the years were, "Scouse Kevin", Pete M, Mike and Pete B, Paul W, "The Cowboy", Phil B, Kirk, Steven C, Terry C, Jeff H, Garry M, Terry P, all the R&H drivers, and anyone else who knew me! And finally all my private regulars of Gordon, Louise, Gary, Stan, Steve, Dave, Bill, Kevin, Dave, Julie, Phil, Tom and Biddy. A special mention to Phil my mechanic who worked on my cars and got them through all the breakdowns and all the strict taxi MOTs!

Dedication

This book is dedicated to my late wife, Leslie Durtnall, without whom my life would have been so much less fulfilled! I was privileged to marry the love of my life, crazy person, soul mate, and the strongest most dignified woman I have ever known! We were destined to be together because of the accidental way in which we literally bumped into each other! We raised two amazing children together, giving them both memorable, loving and secure starts in life! We both retired early to live out our best lives until on 5th July 2020 she was cruelly taken from us by the bastard disease that is Cancer! I will love you always, until we meet again, Adrian xxx

INTRODUCTION

The truth is stranger than fiction! You couldn't make it up! This book covers an amazing thirty-eight years of my life, from age twenty-one to fifty-nine. It was never boring. It was funny, exciting, dramatic, dangerous, entertaining, uplifting, character-building, spiritual, sad and memorable. The inspiration for writing my book has been a therapy in a way for me, since I lost my wife to breast cancer two and a half years ago. I was a taxi driver in Hemel Hempstead for twenty-nine years, from age twenty-four to fifty-three, and through all those years my passengers, after listening to my funny stories, would always say that I should write a book when I retired, so I have! I went from being a shy and quiet young man, to a very confident driver, speaker and self-employed business owner. Every word is true, and all the events actually did happen to me or my friends. I have not named anyone to save them embarrassment, but those who know will know!

CHAPTER 1

MEETING, ENGAGEMENT, MARRIAGE

The first of September 1984, my twenty-first birthday. Fast forward to the evening that was destined to change my life forever.

I had organised a meal for all my friends at a nightclub in the local town that I had never socialised in before. The meal was great and we all got on the dance floor for a good old boogie. MY ROUND! So up to the bar I went. Whilst standing there, I felt a tap on the shoulder. I turned around, and standing there was this blonde bombshell in a tight mini-skirt and white court shoes! Now this sort of thing was totally mind-blowing for me, and suddenly I thought, *Hang on a minute, it's my twenty-first birthday!* So I blurted out, "Are you a strip-o-gram?"

Thankfully, she laughed it off and sat me down for a chat! She said, "I am married, but separated, and I have a three-and-a-half-year-old daughter."

Wow, I was glad I was sitting down as it was a lot to take in, and most blokes would have run a mile! But I was very relaxed about it all and said that I definitely wanted to see her again as she was just too beautiful to let go! We had a few dances and found out that we both loved the same dance music and artists, so we exchanged numbers at the end of the night and I went searching for all my friends that I had abandoned after being seduced by Leslie! When I found them all I could say was, "Did you see her, oh my god, did you see how god damn hot she was!?"

They all laughed and took the mickey out of me and said, "Let's get you home you drunken idiot!"

A few weeks later Leslie actually told me the reason she had tapped me on the shoulder was because the night before she had met someone at the same club and I was a case of mistaken identity! She had both our numbers and luckily for me I was the first to ring her, so she chose me

I think it must have been love at first sight, because seven months after that we were engaged, and then married on 26th October 1985!

To celebrate our upcoming engagement, we booked ourselves a romantic getaway to a sunny resort in Italy right next to Venice. We were like a couple of teenagers, as it was our first time on a flight to another country, and Leslie couldn't wait for the take-off. Of course, being on a budget, we were self-catering, and first job on arrival was the supermarket. As soon as we walked into the shop, our eyes popped out at the display in front of us. Bottles of Asti Spumanti sparkling wine for 26p a bottle! Ha, ha! We didn't have much room for any food in the trolley after seeing that beautiful sight! Back at the holiday apartment, we didn't waste any time in getting our own private party started. There were corks popping and flying everywhere, loud music blaring out and crazy drunk dancing.

Being so close to Venice, it was easy to arrange a boat trip over to the city. Our captain was a really jolly Italian singer, and he serenaded us with his songs as we crossed the sea. I'm sure he had been on the sauce! Venice was lovely; the glass works factory was amazing, and seeing all the gondolas was great fun, but way too expensive for us.

The next day was a rest day on the beach and fun in the sea. Both of us were knackered and we made the fatal mistake of falling asleep on our beach towels. We hadn't put any sun cream on and were burning red! Damn! Back at the apartment, I was shivering with sun stroke, so Leslie went out to get pizza. Of course, not knowing about pizza sizes in Italy, Leslie ordered two (!), and when they came out they were HUGE! We laughed our heads off because each one was about two foot across!

When we got back home to the UK, my mum and dad laid on a great engagement party for us, and everybody was so jealous of our deep tans. Of course, we kept quiet about our little sunburn episode.

Our wedding day was done on a shoestring, as we had limited funds at the time. So it was the registry office, reception and all home-made catering at my mum and dad's house. My wife even made the huge wedding cake that was in the shape of a heart and fed about eighty people. It was the happiest day of our lives and we couldn't stop smiling all day. So in the morning I had terrible nerves, felt ill and wanted to be sick. My wife-to-be was all ready to go in her wedding dress, when somehow she managed to drop a full glass bottle of milk on her foot. Quickly, she had to put her wedding shoes on before her big toe swelled up. Luckily, it wasn't broken, and we just laughed it off, as nothing was going to spoil our big day. My green Ford Capri had the white ribbons tied to the bonnet in a V shape and looked great as we drove off, until just as we arrived at the registry office, when the ribbon detached from the front and blew backwards over the car. Minor details, but very memorable. The registry building was called 'The Bury' and was a lovely eighteenth-century Grade 2-listed house with big gardens, so just brilliant for our wedding photos. Unfortunately, in the last few years the registry office has changed to the new 'Forum' civic centre in the town, and it's nowhere near as special as The Bury. The reception at my mum and dad's house was brilliant, and everybody had a great time at the after party. I made up a special mix-tape with all our favourite dance tracks on and our special wedding song "Careless Whisper" by George Michael, which was very emotional to dance to with Leslie who was now my wife!! My mum was busy taking all our wedding photos and when the album was finished and presented to us a few weeks later, they were just great to look at and see the pure joy and delight in our faces!

CHAPTER 2

NOVICE TAXI DRIVER

So happily married, living in my wife's council house, I read about the 'Right To Buy' scheme. We applied, and were told that with a big discount we could buy our house for £26,300. Even on my low wages at my warehouse job, it was too good an opportunity to miss. With the mortgage arranged to start in September 1987, my wife announced that she was pregnant, and due in September as well. Oh, shit! Double whammy! We need more money from somewhere.

For a long time before, we would be watching television in the evenings, and kept getting interference from the house opposite that was running a base radio for their private hire taxi company. So my wife said, "Go over the road and ask if they need any part-time drivers."

I wasn't very confident with this idea, as I didn't know my way around the town at all, having only lived there for two years; but I thought, *There's no harm in asking!* Two brothers owned the taxi company, and Bill, who lived opposite me, said I could work part-time to get me started. All I had to do was change my car to a four-door, as my current car was a two-door Capri. When I had bought an appropriate car, I just had to rent the taxi radio and aerial each week.

So, that evening, I put a For Sale sign in the car window, and the very next day I got a knock on the door by two blokes in builders' clothes, asking to test drive the Capri. Unfortunately, I was young and naïve. These two builders turned out to be con-artist joyriders who weren't interested in buying the car at all. My Capri was very new at the time and in immaculate condition, so I casually drove these two around the estate for a while and then let them have a drive. Big mistake! As soon as he got behind the wheel, he said that they needed to go on the motorway, because that was where they did most of their driving. I was in the passenger seat, feeling a bit apprehensive, but I really needed to sell the car. So off they went up the M1, foot flat to the floor and getting up to 100mph and flashing cars in the fast lane to move over. I was scared stiff and kept shouting at him to slow down. He was quite calm about it all and just explained that his boss needed a reliable fast car, that he was very impressed with my car and wanted to buy it. We arrived back at my house, and still shaking from the adrenaline, I started to talk about the price of the car and the paperwork, but they just fobbed me off by saying they had to get the OK from their boss, and I never saw them again.

Thankfully, I did eventually sell the car to someone decent, and bought my first four-door saloon hatchback, a Vauxhall Cavalier, that was suitable for private hire taxi driving.

On 16th September 1987, our son was born, and two weeks later I was all kitted out to start my first evening shift. In at the deep end, Friday night!

My very first booking was to the Queens Head, one of the roughest pubs in the town. The big giveaway was that they always had a 'meat wagon' parked outside. They got in my car, and just said, "Queens Head, please."

Very embarrassed, I said, "I don't know where the pub is or how to get there; could you direct me?"

They were very kind and showed me the way. So that was the first pub learned – only about forty to go! Back then, you could just learn on the job. There was no knowledge test, so you could just pick it up as you went, and the radio operator helped a lot as well. It's funny, looking back to when I needed to keep looking at the street map of the town to get to my next booking. I was too slow, and, of course, when you do less jobs you earn less money. There were lots of rough pubs around the town; all of them had their own reputations and serious regulars that I had to get used to, and who had to get to know me, too. There were some really bad pissheads, especially on a Saturday daytime, and a lot of drivers just flatly refused to pick them up, because you would have to literally go into the pub, call their name out and make sure they were ready to leave. The landlord of the pub would point out your customer because they were too pissed to get off their bar stool, and would normally have to be helped out to my car by their friends. If you didn't go in the pub, you would be sitting outside wasting time waiting for them to stagger out.

As I learned the roads and shortcuts, I got around a lot quicker, especially on nights, as the only other cars speeding around were usually taxis. There were no speed cameras or speed humps and the police left us alone, so we had the roads to ourselves. There were lots of police traps back then, looking for drunk drivers, because it was a very big problem and they clamped down on it hard. My passengers loved it, because whenever we got pulled over and the police saw my private hire stickers on my doors, they waved us straight through and you felt like royalty. Years later, and the council decided to do a trial scheme of 'sleeping policemen' speed humps down a fast road near our office, and went a bit overboard by putting in thirteen humps past a big secondary school, which certainly gave everyone living on the isolated housing estate 'The Hump'! Of course, the scheme was deemed a success, was expanded throughout the town and included the introduction of these new 'mini-roundabouts'. We all joked that it was because of our famous 'magic roundabout' being 'the mother of all roundabouts'. So our fast and furious days of bombing about were over, and we all started moaning about the wear and tear on our suspensions.

CHAPTER 3

1987 STORM

After working for three weeks part-time on Thursday, Friday and Saturday evenings, we were all rudely awoken on the morning of 16th October by the terrible storm that had hit overnight with 100mph winds. We had been specifically told the night before by Mr Michael Fish, the weather forecaster, that there wasn't a hurricane coming. My taxi boss, who lived opposite, came rushing over to us and told me to move my car off the street immediately, as his roof tiles were being blown off his house and were crashing into the street next to my car. He didn't have to tell me twice, as I could see the broken tiles in the road. Very quickly, I drove straight around to the back of my house, where I hoped it would be safe.

Like a fool, I thought it would be busy working in the storm. Bad idea! It was chaos. Fallen trees everywhere, traffic jams, roads blocked, everybody's fences flattened, debris in the road that you had to swerve around. I was given a pick-up at a pub out in the countryside. So I set off out through the Old Town, which was clear of traffic, and all of a sudden, THUD! I slowly got out of my car, as I had that horrible sinking feeling that something bad had happened to my car, and there it was. A big dent in the metalwork next to the windscreen, and a lovely crack in the glass as well. I had hit a big branch from a fallen tree that was sticking out in the road. Pissed off, I carried on to my pick-up, and when they got in my car they told me that it was way too dangerous to be out, and I should really go home soon. They had been cutting up fallen trees in a field, and another tree had fallen onto their truck and had written it off. Hence me taking them home. When I got home, I rang my Dad, who was a keen photographer at the time, and he had been out getting shots of the fallen trees. He had come across a car that had been totally flattened by a huge tree.

Apparently, the parents had parked up, gone to get their child, and when they got back, the tree had fallen onto their car. Anyone in that car would have been killed. Good God, how lucky were they?

The wind speed was just ridiculous and made a horrible howling noise all the time, which was very scary for anybody trying to get about. I saw several brick walls that had just collapsed onto pavements, and could have caused serious injury to anyone walking past them. Fence panels were everywhere, including several of mine, but there was no point trying to pick them up because you were just fighting a losing battle against the wind. When I got in and out of my car, I had to hold on tight to the door so that it didn't fly out of my hands and possibly bend the hinges back; and every passenger I picked up I had to make sure they did the same. The storm only lasted a day, but caused wide devastation across London and the south-east, including thousands of trees and millions of pounds of damage to buildings and houses.

CHAPTER 4

NIGHT SHIFTS

Doing a full-time job in Watford, getting home at five thirty p.m., and starting the part-time taxi driving from seven thirty p.m. till midnight, Thursday, Friday and Saturday, was very tiring mentally, because it was all new, and learning the roads by searching on the street map all the time was quite a challenge. After several weeks of driving, I had a bit of a breakdown with the stress of it all, and really thought I couldn't carry on. The only thing that kept me going was the extra money coming in, which we desperately needed to pay the mortgage.

After six months, I had learned the roads properly, and that's when the opportunity came up at my warehouse job for me to take the redundancy they were offering and go full-time taxi-ing.

Working nights was never boring, with rows, arguments, domestics, drunks, fights, swearing, abuse, broken bottles and glass outside the pubs. So, for protection, we would always have our doors locked, and passenger window open slightly to talk to our customers before picking them up. Also, each car had their own radio number. Mine was R18, but our distress call was R13, so when an R13 went out, every available car would drive straight to their location to provide assistance. We had an old boy (about sixty) working for us, a bit skinny and frail, but 'wouldn't hurt a fly' type. Well, one night he picked up two well-known villains from a rough block of flats in his Ford Sierra Estate. Ten minutes later, our operator got a call from a resident of the flats, who said, "I have just seen your driver being KIDNAPPED! They roughed him up and shoved him in the back of his own estate car, where the dog guard is, and DROVE OFF!"

"R13! R13! All cars to attend the incident!"

Oh my God, it all kicked off! It was like a scene from a movie! I thought I was driving fast, but then I got overtaken by 'ALF', the company owner, going like a bat out of hell! Old Bill were everywhere, blues and twos, all our drivers, and EVERY other taxi company in the town were looking for poor old 'R4'. Hours went past, and nothing; nobody could find the car. Then, about two a.m., we got a phone call from the police station of a town twenty-five miles away. 'R4' had been abandoned with his car, so he was able to drive to the local police station and give a full description of the well-known villains. The police quickly drove round to a known address in that town, and arrested both of them on the spot. The police even got all of his money back that had been stolen. RESULT!

My next eventful encounter with the boss, 'ALF', was a multi-booking for several cars at a rather rowdy social club event. We all turned up on time, but no one was coming out, so the boss said, "I will go in and drag them out!"

Five minutes later, he came back out, looking pissed off, and said, "They don't need us any more."

The boss got back in his car, and, just as he shut his door, somebody came running out of the club and threw a fire extinguisher right through his back windscreen, smashing it to pieces. BAD IDEA! I didn't know it at the time, but the boss was a Black Belt in the martial art of Tang-Soo-Do, and the drunk offender didn't stand a chance. He was thrown on his back and had a fist put in his face. I thought the boss was going to kill him. Luckily, the police turned up, and it all ended peacefully. Now that is somebody I want on my side at all times in that situation.

A few more great stories from the boss, 'ALF':

A driver-in-distress call, 'R13', went out during the day for an incident in a quiet side street. Many of our drivers turned up and were met by two hooligans arguing with the driver and being very aggressive. The boss pushed his way to the front of the crowd and straight away grabbed one of them by the throat. The other idiot then leaned into the back seat of the taxi and pulled out a shotgun. He then smacked the boss around the face with the barrel of the shotgun, but straight away in return he was punched in the face by the boss, and was knocked out stone cold. The police turned up twenty minutes later and were going to arrest my boss for assault, until all the witnesses explained about the shotgun. The idiot with the shotgun was deservedly sent to prison for five years.

CHAPTER 5

GYPSIES

There was a purpose-built, permanent gypsy caravan site a few miles out of town that all the drivers knew about, and they would never drive onto the site for safety reasons. So one evening, the boss unfortunately ended up with some gypsies in his car who had paid up front to get home. Of course, they were going to this very site out of town, and the boss had told them in no uncertain terms that he would only drop them at the entrance. So, at the entrance to the site, the obvious argument started. After a while, they got out of the car, but the last passenger had got the right hump and pulled out a knife. He said, "Look, I've got a knife and I am going to put it through the back of your seat. What are you going to do about that, then?"

So the boss turned round and punched him in the mouth, and knocked all his teeth out. Ha, ha! Brilliant!

All the drivers were very cautious when they were around the gypsies, as, unfortunately, their reputation preceded them for being disruptive and hard to deal with. If ever there was a gypsy funeral due to be in the town, nearly all the pubs would shut for the night, and hardly any taxis would work that night. There was always one pub that would risk staying open for the funeral wake, and the landlord was paid well in advance for all drinks and any damage that happened if any fights broke out. Of course, there was always trouble, and the offenders were told afterwards: Never again!

One taxi driver had his car stolen off his driveway, but a few days later he learned from an anonymous tip-off that the gypsies had stolen it for joyriding, and it was parked inside the gypsy caravan site. Now this caravan site was a very intimidating place to enter, and the police wouldn't even go there unless they had an armed response unit with them. Well, my mate was six foot five, very well known by the gypsy elders, and didn't mess around when he was pissed off. So, bold as brass, he went marching straight onto the caravan site and demanded to know where his car was. A bunch of lads showed him around a corner, and there was his car, in better condition than when it was taken. It had been washed and cleaned inside and out, a puncture repaired and new wiper blades fitted. I think the respectful elders had given the lads a bollocking, and made them put everything right.

As I've said before, our gypsy community seem to have their own set of rules, and do what they want to wind people up. I have had many run-ins with the gypsies, and it was normally the teenagers. One lovely summer's evening, all of us on the taxi rank were having a chat and a laugh, when a car came driving slowly through the pedestrianised zone, and as they passed us they threw their milkshakes at us, hitting me square in the chest. I was covered in strawberry milkshake, and bloody fuming. Then the bastards stopped twenty feet away and started taunting us because we couldn't chase them, as we were all boxed in waiting on the rank. Typical arsehole behaviour!

CHAPTER 6

DRUNKS

So I arrived at a shopping centre for a booking. A tipsy teenage girl gave me the right name and got in the front, but before I could look, more tipsy teenage girls bundled in the back. Oh, shit! This wasn't going to be fun, as there were four in the back, making five in total. I wasn't going anywhere, but try telling that to five drunk teenage girls. It was a nightmare. I got on the radio and told the operator to call the police as they wouldn't leave the car, and I was really angry by now. Then it happened.

Whoosh! Whoosh! All four of them in the back had sprayed all of their Coke cans EVERYWHERE! What a bloody mess: sticky Coke all over me, and the whole interior of the car. I don't know what I would have done if I had caught one of them when they legged it. All I could do was go back to the office to calm down, and clean up the mess. Another bitter pill to swallow.

Christmas and New Year were always huge earners, of course, and I could work more hours as I had booked holiday time off from my warehouse job. Everyone was always happy and in good spirits at this time of year, and it was good fun to work.

BUT the 'seasonal' drinkers at this time of year couldn't hold their drink, and we had to deal with a lot of rowdy passengers at kicking-out time. There would be lots of office parties, every day for all of December, so all the social clubs would be packed with office workers taking advantage of the free bars. Drunks could be hilariously funny sometimes, especially when you dropped them off at their destination. They were fine sitting in the car, but when they opened the passenger door and tried to walk, most of them staggered and wobbled, or tried to hold on to the car bonnet to keep their balance. One bloke did this and managed to get safely to the kerb, and waved goodbye to me as I drove off. I looked in my mirror just as he fell backwards down a flight of stairs that led to a basement! Oh, shit! After laughing my head off, I turned around to go back and check on him. He was OK and just staggered through his door.

Another similar drunk was banging on his front door, and peeing in his front garden. When the door opened, the angry resident had to show him to his correct house two doors down. Ha, ha, he had been peeing in his neighbour's front garden!

The worst drunks were the ones that passed out and were on their own. So, if you didn't know where they lived, the only solution was to drive to the police station, park outside, and the officers would get the drunk out of the car for us and gave them a place to sleep it off.

New Year's Eve was always a strange one to work, because a lot of people had house parties or were in the clubs early, so it all went quiet by about nine p.m. So I would go home until midnight, and then, of course, it would go mental for about four hours straight. Our extra earnings over the festive season would usually pay for our summer holidays.

CHAPTER 7

PRIVATE HIRE

Six months of part-time taxi driving and I was hooked. My full-time job was relocating, so I took the £2000 redundancy money they were offering, and paid off the loan I had used to buy my first car. It was a Vauxhall Cavalier and was suitable to be a private hire taxi. After my leaving party at work, I rushed home and prepared to go full-time taxi driving the very next day. I worked seven days straight, eight hours a night, and earned more than I did in a month at my old job. RESULT!

Of course, working a lot of hours in the evenings, I would get hungry, so Leslie would make me a huge lunchbox of food and a flask of hot drink which just about fitted under my seat. When the other drivers saw my feast of sandwiches, cakes and biscuits, they were extremely jealous and said I had the best wife ever.

One of the golden rules that we had drummed into us from the start was, 'Only four passengers maximum, as that is our insurance cover limit. Never five!' People would try it on, and it caused a few arguments, but generally everyone knew the rules. One day, a day-time driver who had a taxi licensed to carry five, took them all to an out-of-town venue, and said another car would pick them up in the evening. Unfortunately, this day driver didn't mention the fifth passenger, and when the boss went to pick them up, he was met by five angry passengers, and he was only insured to carry four. After a lot of arguing, the only solution was to hide the extra passenger in the boot. The next day, the boss gave the day driver a severe tongue-lashing for putting him in that awkward position.

For a few months, I worked the night shift right through to six a.m. One Sunday morning, I was sitting in the office as the day shift were arriving, and a group of angry people phoned up to say they were waiting in London to be picked up, and the car which took them there hadn't arrived. This particular driver couldn't be traced, so somebody had to volunteer to go and pick them up. All the day shift had bookings to do, so muggins got the short straw! We explained on the phone that I would be there to pick them up in forty-five minutes, and they agreed to wait for me. I was five minutes away from the pick-up point in London, when they told me over the radio that the passengers couldn't wait any longer as they were cold and wet, and had jumped in another cab. I was fuming. I was cursing the whole way home. I stormed into the office and demanded payment from somebody for all my wasted efforts. The boss agreed to a week's free radio rental and £20 cash. No more volunteering for me!

My first car only lasted about a year, as back then I was clocking up fifty thousand taxi miles a year. The engine developed a small oil leak and I couldn't see where it was coming from, plus it was burning a lot of oil as well. I kept topping it up constantly, until, a few weeks later, I was just travelling up towards the bypass, and the car just stopped dead. The AA examined the car at the roadside and told me the bad news. The engine had seized up! Oops, time for a new car.

My next car was another Vauxhall Cavalier, which again only lasted about a year, with the extreme mileage taking its toll on the car, so I traded it in for a brand new Ford Orion diesel. That car was great and lasted me for five and a half years, clocking up a huge two hundred and sixty-three thousand miles. When it got to forty-eight thousand miles, it was running like a dream, until one day, without warning, as I was pulling out of a turning, I just heard a quiet 'ping' and the engine just stopped dead. Oh, bugger, now what could that be? It turned out that the cam belt had snapped and bent four valves! I wasn't happy because the belt was due to be changed at fifty thousand miles. Luckily, our taxi company mechanic rebuilt the engine for me in a few days and all was as good as new.

I was young, enthusiastic, confident and game for a laugh, and to prove it, I did something which seems a bit outrageous now, but it makes a brilliant story. So, it was a quiet Tuesday night, and the operator said, "Anyone want to take two Chinese businessmen to the next big town, wait and return? Details are in the office."

I volunteered, but everybody was laughing in the office when I got there. The joke was that these two businessmen each wanted to use the services of a prostitute!

"Hell, yeah, I'm up for that!"

I got to the pub and the landlord gave me precise instructions on which road to travel down and what to say.

Oh my God! Kerb-crawling – that's a new one for the CV! So the two Chinese men got in, and off we went. We got to the correct street, and I slowed down with my passenger window open. A young girl approached my window, and I told her that I had two Chinese gentlemen in the back that needed looking after. She said, "No problem, I'll do them BOTH!" She got in, and we drove round to her flat, where she took the first one inside. Fifteen minutes later, he came out with a great big grin on his face, and then she took the second one in. Fifteen minutes later, a big grin on his face, and mission completed. Driving back to the pub I kept thinking about what I had just done, shaking my head in disbelief and laughing to myself! When I got back to the pub the landlord came out and shook my hand. He said I did a great job and was laughing with me at how daring and risky it all was! Of course when I got back to the office all the drivers wanted to know all the details and if it was easy to actually get away with it. I just said if I was questioned by anybody I was just a driver doing what I was instructed and completely innocent! I've lost count of the number of times I have re-told that amazing story to all my passengers!

Driving around late at night, you certainly see a lot of strange sights. One night, at about two a.m., I was driving back to town through a big forest, and was busting for a pee, so I dived behind a hedge and started peeing. While I was doing this, I casually looked around and, to my amusement, I could see about six cars in the dark, all with steamed-up windows, bouncing up and down and with moaning and groaning going on.

Oh my God! It's a dogging site! Ha, ha! This was before phone cameras were around. I would have loved to have videoed it, ha, ha! No one knew I was there because they were all too busy bonking. I made a hasty retreat and didn't look back.

Being a Private Hire driver means you could only pick up pre-booked fares, and not flag-downs. The way around this was a practice called 'blagging', where you parked up outside venues and clubs, and if someone got in, you just called it in to the operator, and she put it down as a booking. One night, I got a bit greedy, I suppose, and was a victim of my own success. Over the course of a couple of hours, I managed to do about six different fares, and couldn't believe my luck. Every time I came back to the front of the club, someone would tap on my window to ask if I was available. The club I chose to blag from was too close to the official Taxi Rank, and they were watching me like hawks. One of them decided to pull up alongside me and gave me a very strong tongue-lashing. The next morning, my next-door neighbor banged on my door to tell me I had two flat tyres. On closer examination, I realised they had been slashed with a Stanley knife! There was no need to call the police, as it was obvious who had done it. The Taxi Rank cars had taken out retribution on me. Lesson learned!

Back in the days before mobile phones and the internet, the pubs would be a huge social meeting place for all the builders and trades people, where they would give jobs and contracts to each other by word of mouth. Every Friday afternoon all the bosses would pay out all their workers in cash at the local pub and arrange work schedules for the following week. If they needed extra workers then they would use us to ferry them around the other pubs recruiting who they needed! As the town pubs were so spread out amongst all the hills and different estates we were constantly ferrying people between pubs to find their mates!

When there were major sporting events on, especially during the Euros or World Cup, I would have the games on the radio, with Jonathan Pearce commentating on Capital Gold. Everyone listened with excitement to his amazing commentary, and when we scored, his passion and enthusiasm was just brilliant. It was a great atmosphere in the car, and better than watching it on the telly.

Working nights and knowing lots of well-off people always had its perks, and I was always getting invites to after-show parties and events. On one occasion, it was the night of the Mike Tyson *v* Frank Bruno fight in Las Vegas, and it started about three a.m. It was a huge sporting event, and everybody wanted to watch it; but it was an expensive pay-per-view event. Luckily, I picked up my millionaire mate, and got an invite for four drivers to watch the fight at his mansion. WOW! What a night, even though Bruno lost. We had all been drinking, and it was about five a.m. The host piped up, "I'm getting some prostitutes now; who's in?" TIME TO GO! We all made our excuses, shook hands and left to go back to our wives.

CHAPTER 8

CELEBRITIES

One of the perks of this job was picking up famous people or celebrities, and my turn came one evening when a well-known footballer in the town wanted picking up from a pub. So I piped up, "Let me pick him up, because I actually went to school with him and he will remember me!" Oh my God! It was brilliant talking to him about the old school days, and naming all the teachers we had. Our school was in the countryside and next to a working farm, and to get to the football pitches and running tracks, everyone had to walk along next to the cows and all their slurry rivers of wet cow shit. So you've guessed already, occasionally the odd poor boy would get attacked and thrown in the cow slurry! Well, it was common knowledge that my famous friend had been one of the unfortunate few to be unceremoniously thrown in the cow dip by his so-called school friends. I gleefully reminded him of this fact; he remembered it very well and laughed out loud at the thought of it. We went round picking up his other professional football mates, who were part of the original 'Crazy Gang', and I listened to all their mad stories and high jinx. He had a reputation of being a hard nut, but he explained to me that was just his extreme enthusiasm he had for everything he did in life, and which drove him on to be successful in everything new he tried. I gave him my mobile number and he used me all the time after that. Any parties or events he had, I was always asked to ferry his guests back and forth. So, when he got married, I was in big demand after the reception. I got so busy that I had to call all my taxi mates to help out. It certainly was a big event, and you could hear the music blaring out, and even the man himself on the karaoke! After his football career finished, he got a lucky break in the film industry, and became very successful at acting!

He used our big cinema and nightclubs to hold the premiere of one of his big action films, and lots of celebrities turned up that night. I was working on the taxi rank, and when I got to the front, we would all talk in a group about who we had taken home that night. A lot of the guests were footballers and *EastEnders* actors. Well, I got an *EastEnders* legend and his 'girlfriend', not his wife! "Take us to this hotel, please!" Unfortunately, I didn't get to speak to him, as he was too busy snogging the face off this young groupie!

Another evening, I picked up from a big house on the posh estate, and as soon as she got in with her boyfriend, I recognised her straight away as a 'Page 3' model, even with all her clothes on! "Stringfellows in London, please, driver." I dropped them off outside the club, and noticed the bright yellow dress she was just about wearing! "Please pick us up at three a.m. and take us back home."

I got to the club early for the return trip, and it was very entertaining and exciting watching all the different stars and celebrities staggering out of Stringfellows into their waiting limos. My return trip had a huge diversion because their other celebrity friends needed dropping home in Marlow first. Of course there were no sat-navs back then so they helped me with directions even though they were all absolutely hammered!

The very next day, I went into the newsagents, and there she was on the front cover of a popular newspaper, staggering out of the club wearing that very distinctive yellow dress!

A normal-looking middle-aged woman got in my car with her food shopping, and in a Welsh accent she said, "Do you mind taking me out of town to a big country house in one of the villages?"

I said, "Of course, no problem at all. Are you staying there for a while, then?"

That was when she let the cat out of the bag. "I'm just here for the day to do some filming for *Little Britain*. I'm the Welsh barmaid in the series."

"Oh, wow! I'm a big fan of the show, it's absolutely hilarious!"

She then said, "David and Matt will be in their posh fat women suits today, so it's going to be very funny; and then I'll be doing my sketch with Matt as the only gay in the village." I could have chatted to her all day, but we got to the film set and I had to say goodbye.

For my fiftieth birthday, one of my treats was a trip up to the Emirates Stadium with my son, to do the guided tour led by Arsenal legend Nigel Winterburn. Arsenal had won the FA Cup just a few months before, so our first stop was the trophy room with every single cup the club had won, and then special photo-shoots with the FA Cup of that year. Nigel was a great host and we got to talk to him a lot as he was showing us around the dressing room, with all the players' shirts hanging up where they would sit for the pre-match talk from Arsene Wenger. Next was the press conference room, where you could sit in Arsene's chair for photos and pretend to take questions from the press. We all took turns to sit in the big chairs in the dugout, where all the substitutes sit, and Nigel took a question-and-answer session from our group, before we all retired to the club bar and lounge for food and drinks. Afterwards, my son said he would try and get us tickets to go and see a match at the stadium.

My wife, Leslie, was an extremely talented lady; from accomplished free-hand artist, wedding and celebration cake-maker and specialist decorator, fantastic cook, silver service waitress, beautician and nail expert, children's entertainer and independent mum, to self-employed business owner of 'Tips & Toes' nail extensions and beauty treatments, which she ran from our converted conservatory at home.

One day, Leslie was chatting to one of her nail clients about all her artwork she had drawn, and was showing the lady a few of her favourites. The lady then casually mentioned to Leslie that her brother was a well-known freehand artist who would love her work. His name was Charles Bronson, the infamous prisoner! The lady asked if she could show Charles her work as he would probably do a couple for Leslie in return. Sure enough, about a month later, the lady came back with two signed drawings from Charles Bronson, saying that he had told her that some day they would be worth a lot of money! Leslie was gobsmacked, as you can imagine.

CHAPTER 9

ARSEHOLES

Nightclub returns were very popular back then. The drivers were paid up-front for both journeys to an out-of-town nightclub. Our rule was that if they were more than fifteen minutes late, then we would leave them there, as they might have got lucky, pulled and got a one-night stand. Sometimes, if you hung around for a bit, you could blag a fare back to town. This was very risky, because undercover detectives would get you to pick them up, pay you and then arrest you. So, usually, if there was a group of women, then it was safe.

Most customers were regulars, and this trip was just that. Two of the four passengers were very well-known regulars of mine, but the other two turned out to be right arseholes! We were going to a club about fifteen miles away, which meant going on the motorway. Whilst doing 70mph, I was fully concentrating on the road, as you do, when suddenly they opened the back window and said, "We just need some fresh air!" – and then they started laughing.

We got to the club, and they all got out. I turned to my left to reverse out, and then the penny dropped: my f'ing passenger headrest was missing. Right, I'll get the little shits on the way back! I waited at the club for the return trip, but only my good friend turned up, and he couldn't apologise enough. He promised me they would replace the headrest, as the arseholes who did it worked at a garage. Two months later, and no replacement headrest. So you know the saying, 'Hell hath no fury like a woman scorned!'

My wife screamed at me, "Take me to that garage NOW! I'm giving that little shit a piece of my mind!"

My wife stormed into their boss's office and told him about the drunken antics, and almost got them both sacked. I got paid for a replacement headrest and all was sorted. The very next day, I also bought my wife a huge bunch of flowers.

Traffic wardens are everyone's pet hate, and I have had quite a few arguments with them over the years. Our taxi rank in the town was very long, and occasionally, if a driver needed to pop into the shops to buy something, they would just park up at the very back of the rank out of the way, and the rest of the drivers would just drive around them until they got back. Now officially you were not allowed to leave your taxi unattended on the rank, but this practice had been going on for years without any problems, and amongst all of the drivers it was just considered a perk of the job. Well, some arsehole must have complained to the council about this, and they decided to clamp down on this practice. One day, I parked on the back of the rank, because it was a quiet day and I needed to go clothes shopping in Primark. As I was walking back down an alley towards my car, I could see a traffic warden sniffing around my car and taking photos of my wheels. I quickly put my bags of shopping in my boot without him seeing and shouted at him, "Oi, what the hell are you doing? I'm allowed to park on the taxi rank!"

His reply was, "We have been instructed by the council to book any unattended taxis on the rank, and your car hasn't moved for thirty minutes, because I took a photo of your wheels twenty-five minutes ago, and it hasn't moved."

I quickly had to think of a good excuse, and I came up with this: "Well, Mr Warden, the reason I parked here is because I had an elderly woman passenger in my car who needed my assistance to get to Marks and Spencer to order all her Christmas food and buy presents, and then her daughter turned up late to help her carry on with her shopping trip."

The warden gave me a strong warning and said he would report the incident to the town hall; but luckily I didn't get a ticket and heard nothing from the town hall.

I was told many years ago that if you ever get a parking ticket, you should ALWAYS contest it in writing. If you put forward a good enough argument, it will get rescinded, because it might be your first offence or the warden didn't issue it properly.

My wife was disabled and had a Blue Badge, which was great for parking on double yellow lines up to three hours. What I didn't know was that the rules were different in London. We had an important medical appointment in London and were running late, as usual, because of the traffic. I found what I thought was a suitable parking space, and because there were no wardens around to ask, I just had to gamble. Of course, when we got back to the car, there on the windscreen was the dreaded parking ticket and the offending warden just walking off. I shouted at him because we had displayed our Blue Badge correctly, but he explained that we should have applied for the London exemption badge, and to make sure we did that in good time before our next trip into London. Of course, I pleaded my innocence to all of this when I contested the ticket, and they very kindly rescinded it as it was my first offence in their district.

Parking at the UCLH Hospital in London was normally fine, if you could find a free disabled parking bay. One day, we were really struggling to find a suitable bay and waiting on a double yellow line for a space to free up. I got a tap on the window from a security guard and I thought he was going to move us away, but instead the lovely man had seen our struggle and directed us to the private underground car park that had disabled bays, and as long as we got an exemption form from reception, we were good to park there. RESULT!

We had just got back from a lovely two-week holiday and decided to go on a shopping trip in the next town. We parked in our usual spot on the high street, put our Blue Badge up and spent a couple of hours in the shopping centre. As we approached our car to go home, we noticed a police officer and a traffic warden standing around our car. Of course, we were quite bemused by this and asked what the problem was.

The warden explained that my wife's Blue Badge had expired a week ago. Oops! We explained about the holiday and that we hadn't even looked at the badge for ages. I apologised sincerely for our oversight and said I would renew it straight away. The warden and police officer accepted our explanation and let us go on our way.

CHAPTER 10

RUNNERS

One lesson you learned very quickly was how to minimise the risk of having a 'runner', by taking money up-front on longer trips, going out of town, or going to dodgy areas. Most people you just had to trust, but when it rarely happened, it was very annoying. On one occasion, after picking up from a nightclub, I was stopped and waiting for my money from the front passenger, when he opened the door and started to get out! "OI, DICKHEAD!" I shouted, and ran after him.

To my surprise, and his, I actually caught him (first time ever!). Luckily, he hadn't run far, so I could still keep an eye on my car, which had both doors wide open and the engine still running. So I thought, *Now what do I do? Is it really worth it for a £5 fare, when it's really busy back at the rank?* So I punched him in the face and threw him in the hedge! "Don't ever do that again, shithead!" I was quite angry at the time and the adrenaline just got the better of me; but on later reflection, I found it quite funny and thought to myself, *Don't mess with Big Ade, because you'll come off worse!*

It was midnight, and I got a call from a hotel to take a young lad to the city. I told him it was going to be £50 upfront, but as he only had £10 on him, he said, "My brother has money at his house, and I will leave my belongings in the car while I get it off him."

I should have said no, but I'd had a crap night, so I reluctantly agreed, as it was a big fare. So he sat in the back with all his gear, and didn't say much the whole trip, which is quite unnerving. We got to his brother's house, but he wasn't in, so we tried another address, but nothing. I'd had enough by now, so I slowed down next to a police car, which had his blue lights on, talking to another driver. "Excuse me, officer, my passenger hasn't got the money to pay his fare. Can you help me?"

As soon as the officer approached the back door, my passenger was off like a flash, and left all his gear in the car. We both chased after him, but he was like a gazelle and headed towards some woods. Before we started our chase, the police had called for back-up. They arrived in three cars with big searchlights, and surrounded the woods on all sides to cut him off. An hour went by, but nothing. The police said he had probably gone to ground, hiding somewhere. I thanked them all for their amazing response to my situation, and reluctantly set off back home.

CHAPTER 11

SNOW, WIND, RAIN, ICE AND FOG

Driving in all weathers was very challenging, and sometimes downright scary. I started my shift at four p.m., and the fog was like pea soup. I knew where I was by the road names, but I couldn't see the road junctions until I was right on top of them. So I was driving all night in a bubble about ten feet around my car, and my eyes were on stalks because of concentrating so much. Parked cars were dodgy as hell as they had no lights on them, and looking for door numbers was impossible. I literally had to get out of my car to get a closer look at the door numbers. My passengers were amazed at my driving skills, and how I knew where I was going without any landmarks. It was fine driving around town slowly, street by street, until you got to your destination, but any driving out of town through the lanes was scary as hell and it was easy to get lost because everything looked the same. Just hedges both sides and no landmarks. You would have to blast your horn on the sharp bends and hope there wasn't a car coming.

Rain was a blessing and a curse for us. Obviously, when it rained we got very busy when I was working my night shifts, but day shifts at the supermarket were horrible.

Having to load the boot up and carry all the shopping to people's houses in the pouring rain was no joke, plus everyone in the car would steam up all the windows with condensation, so driving around was even harder. Even in the summer you could get caught out with the heavy showers, so when you were dressed in just shorts and T-shirts, you could get soaked through quite easily carrying the shopping a long way. If it rained too heavily, then the roads would start to flood in all the usual places, running down all the hills and causing big jams wherever it flooded. One road I got to was so bad that I had to wait my turn to go through, and just rev the bollocks off the engine to stop any water going up the exhaust until we reached the other side.

We had lots of fun driving in the snow, practising our handbrake turns in the car parks, and turning corners quicker with the handbrake as well. A lot of my cars were front-wheel drive, which were excellent for grip in the snow. Any big cars like Mercedes or Jaguars were crap in the snow and I would leave them standing at junctions. Our town was very hilly, so rush hours were crazy, with stupid drivers stopping on hills, getting stuck, and causing massive jams. I saw some drivers with four-wheel drive Range Rovers charging £20 a time to tow stranded cars up the hills. Nice little earner! If it was too bad on the hills, we would just have to go the flat route, even if it was twice as long, but nobody cared as long as we got there safely. One night it was -10 outside, and I was driving along a country lane. I went round a bend and the car spun sideways, leaving me facing the hedge front and back by inches. After a ten-point turn to get straight again, I was now running late. My mate rang me to say, "I have left the house party, and I am walking down the lane." Two seconds later I saw him, but couldn't stop because of the ice, and I went flashing past him! He came running up to me and said, "You knobhead, you just ran over my foot!"

"Well, if you'd just stayed where you were then you'd be just fine! Ha, ha!"

He saw the funny side of it and he was just glad to get home.

Whenever the snow was around, all the kids would have days off school and hit the big hillsides for the sledging and snowball fights. Unfortunately for us, a very popular road through the suburbs ran right next to the top of the biggest snow slope in the town. So when we drove past the school kids waiting at the top, we would get bombarded with snowballs. This was very alarming for our passengers, and also very dangerous, so the police had to be called to stop them targeting cars, and told to only hit each other. As our town was so bloody hilly, trying to get to people's houses with their shopping was sometimes just too dangerous in the snow. Because of our detailed knowledge of the streets, we could tell as soon as someone gave us their address how difficult it would be to actually get there, and we would have to tell them about the danger of getting stuck in a cul-de-sac, or at the bottom of a hill where I couldn't get back up again. Parked cars on both sides of the street were a nightmare, because one false move and you might slide sideways into them.

One cold winter's day, around about midday, I was just sitting outside a supermarket in the town, waiting to pick up my wife and our friend with all their shopping, when a severe weather alert came over the local radio station about a blizzard coming our way which could dump up to eight inches of snow. I quickly ran into the store to hurry my wife and friend up, and then we quickly drove home. We settled down in the conservatory with our hot chocolates and watched with amazement and huge relief when the sky turned bright white and the blizzard hit, and it didn't let up for about six hours, dumping seven inches of snow and causing chaos around the town, with gridlocked traffic everywhere. I normally gave our friend a lift home as she lived a mile and a half away at the bottom of the hill in the town, but today was just impossible. She walked home and later said that she was walking quicker than the traffic, and she is a slow walker.

About a week earlier, my wife had bought a huge professional doll's house kit in flat-pack form, so now was the perfect time to build and glue it all together. This project went on to be a huge labour of love for many years after and has pride of place in our front room.

CHAPTER 12

HACKNEY CARRIAGE AND HOLIDAYS

Terrorism was always a big concern. We had heard stories of drivers being kidnapped and made to drive car bombs into the city. Then came all the bomb attacks in London, and it made us all very alert as to who we were picking up on certain occasions. My brother-in-law had a chauffeuring business, and a lot of his time was spent in and around London, where he would be waiting outside restaurants, hotels and venues while the IRA bombing campaigns were going on. Like the rest of us, he had no choice about where and when his clients needed his services, and just had to carry on regardless. I suppose that is the nature of terrorism, in that normal every-day people are just going about their daily lives and doing their jobs, and these terrorists are trying to put fear into our lives by using these bombs indiscriminately.

Just something else to worry about, another day at the office.

In 1995, I passed my Hackney Carriage Knowledge test. Normally, the Knowledge test would be very difficult to pass, because not only do you have to answer many questions about start point A to destination point B, but, of course, it has to be the shortest distance and you have to name every street along that route. Then there are questions about where pubs, restaurants, public buildings, train stations, old people's homes, shops, garages and many more were. Luckily for me, I had already been working for eight years on Private Hire, so I managed to get the required pass mark and obtain my Hackney Carriage licence. After this massive achievement, I left my private hire company to go totally independent.

Next was a new car, a Rover 820 diesel saloon, which was lovely to drive, and was very reliable. Three months later, whilst turning right into a car park, a woman on a motorbike slammed into the side of the car, and almost wrote it off. The insurance paid for the extensive repairs, and I was back on the road again. During the three weeks of repair, I had to rent another taxi in a hurry. So I ended up with a crappy and abused Austin Montego. This was very embarrassing when I had to pick up some of my business clients from the airport, who were used to my luxury Rover.

Six months later, we did a family outing to Chessington World of Adventures, and had a brilliant day in the sunshine. The car park had been overflowing, so we had parked on the grass as directed, which turned out to be disastrous. Unknown to me, my engine had a water leak, and it had been soaked up by the grass, so I couldn't see it. If we had parked on tarmac, I would have seen the water leak under the car. So, five miles up the motorway, the engine overheated badly and we got towed home by the AA. My nephew Justin, who was a trained mechanic, stripped the engine down and gave me the bad news that it would cost £500 to rebuild the engine, or a new one would cost £10,000! Luckily, a friend of mine who was only working part-time said I could rent his taxi for a week while mine was being repaired. One engine build later, I was advised to get rid of the car as soon as possible. Luckily, the car was on Hire Purchase, which meant if you had paid half of the instalments you could just hand the car back and the arrangement was finished. I contacted my finance company to arrange collection of my car, and they collected it two days later. So problem solved. All I had to do was buy another car. Luckily, one of my taxi mates was just changing cars, so I bought his old car off him for £800. It was a Vauxhall Senator 3-litre, which was a bit juicy but got me back on the road again.

With mobile phones becoming popular, it was very easy to build up my own private regulars. I would work on the principle of immediate bookings, depending on where I was at the time. My regulars loved my reliable service to get them home whenever they called me; even on Christmas Eve or New Year's Eve, I could be at their venue in five to ten minutes.

Because I worked every weekend, I became extremely reliable for all my regulars, and they would always phone me to take them from their house, between different pubs and then home at the end of the night. I had a group of three brothers, Stan, Steve, and Dave, their wives and girlfriends, Kevin, Bill, Gary, Gordon, Louise and all their friends, who together made up a huge social group and were all out and about at various pubs, clubs, events, parties, barbecues, and restaurants, not just at weekends but weekdays as well! So between them they would keep me very busy. They relied on me so much that I would pick them up anytime, anywhere, from all sorts of strange places, even the middle of a field once! The only time that I couldn't pick Gordon and his mates up was when they rang me from Great Yarmouth after being on a weekend bender, and needed to get back to Hemel before early closing on a Sunday! That was just too much for me as I was very tired from the previous night shift, so they got a local Yarmouth Taxi instead!

My very good friend, Bill, was a huge Chelsea fan and whenever they were playing Arsenal on a Sunday, I would go down to The White Lion in Apsley to watch the game with him and all my other regulars. This was in the time of Thiery Henry and he was just such an amazing player for Arsenal. He scored some brilliant goals and it was always a brilliant laugh taking the piss out of my Chelsea mates if we won! I had other groups of great friends and regulars from certain pubs where my mobile number was passed on to their friends in the pub. The Anchor pub in Beechfield road, then changed to The Leinster and run by Sean the landlord, was the local to Dave, Julie, Phil, Biddy and Tom, who together were another great social group at the weekends for me. Sean later moved up to The Greenacres in Grovehill, and only a few months ago after not seeing him for about ten years, I walked into his pub with Russell to watch an England game and he recognised me straight away and shook my hand, what a legend!

A huge leisure complex with a cinema, restaurants, bars and two nightclubs opened up in 1995, and it was a goldmine for about thirty regular taxis every night. People would travel from miles around to experience this new complex. Because it was built on the edge of town, the only way to get there from the town was by taxi. So early evenings were non-stop, ferrying people to the complex and then taking everyone home later. Every other fare was out of town, and it was just mentally busy. I worked most nights from the complex for twelve years, until the clubs and bars shut down because of all the trouble they attracted, especially at the drive-through McDonald's! Everyone would get their takeaway food and expect us to allow them in our cars. All the drivers agreed to ban food, so people would have to eat it first before going home. A few asked to go into the drive-through, but were not happy when the meter clocked up too much waiting time. I would always warn people about the extra costs of going that route, or just flatly refuse.

In the first year the complex was open, I managed to save enough money to pay for our three-week family holiday at Walt Disney World in Florida. That was an amazing experience, with lots of great memories! The day we arrived, our hire car was pre-booked and waiting for us to drive to our resort. Of course, there were no satnavs back then and I got lost! Every time I missed our turning, we had to go through a toll booth, turn around and come back through the toll booth again. Eventually, I got the right turning and we all cheered! We staggered our theme park days with rest days in between, to go to the water parks, shows, shopping, or fishing on a boat with my best friend Andy. So, on one of our fishing trips to a massive lake nearby, we hired a boat with an outboard motor on it. We set off across the lake, and had a lovely couple of hours' fishing in the middle of the lake. We packed up our fishing gear and went off exploring the far side of the lake, near to all the massive lakeside houses with all their big speed boats moored up on their jetties. Then disaster struck and the throttle link on our engine broke. So our only option was to get the paddles out and row to a couple of young lads who were working on a huge powerboat. They knew the fishing boat man, and offered us a lift back to shore on their boat. Oh my God! What a ride!

When he opened up the throttle on that beast, my cap blew off in the wind, but I didn't care, as I was enjoying the wild ride too much. The fishing boat man was so concerned about us that he didn't charge us at all for the boat rental. Result!

On a different holiday to Tenerife, my mate Andy was with us again and gave me the best laugh ever. We all decided to go to the evening's entertainment, which was a hypnotist show. I was quite a shy guy back then, but I volunteered to get on stage with the other selected audience members. The hypnotist just clicked his fingers and we all went under his spell. Oh my God! First of all, I was back at school, bickering with the man next to me over a stolen rubber and pencil; then I was up dancing like Michael Jackson, with my hand over my crotch! But the worst experience was when I thought the roof was going to collapse if I didn't pull on an imaginary rope in the aisle amongst the audience! I was screaming at everyone to pull on this imaginary rope, and couldn't understand why everyone was in hysterics at my actions. When I got back to my seat, all my holiday friends were just open-mouthed and flabbergasted at what they had just witnessed. I remembered doing it all, but had absolutely no control over it – a bit like being drunk and losing all your inhibitions.

The next evening, my wife wanted to have a go, but we thought it might be dangerous because of her balance problems. How wrong we were! My wife sat on the chairs with everyone else and went under after the click of his fingers. He knew about her condition, but to our amazement he made her get up out of her chair, and she just stood there bolt upright without even wobbling! Next, he had her dancing, doing funny stuff, and then told her she was in a horse race and had won all the money. She then proceeded to stuff all the imaginary notes down her bra! We were just blown away with all of this and kept shaking our heads in disbelief. When she got back to her seat with us, she was so excited and couldn't stop laughing.

So, after a fantastic night and lots of drinks after the show, we all staggered back to our poolside apartments. My mate Andy shouted over to me that he wanted to go for a swim in the pool, so I said, "Yeah, sure, let me get changed into my swimming shorts."

But Andy had different ideas, and instead he jumped into the pool fully clothed, including his brand new suede shoes. Oh my God! I have never laughed so much in my entire life. I just collapsed on the poolside, and my tummy was just hurting so much with laughter.

The security guard came running and we had to drag Andy out of the pool because he wasn't a very good swimmer. Just to make matters worse, he decided to wander off soaking wet through, to try and get into the nightclub. He did manage to get into the club and was just paying for his drinks with soggy notes, when his girlfriend stormed in and dragged him out by his ear. Needless to say, he stayed off the local strong beer for the rest of the holiday.

I always liked to go abroad for my birthday in September, so for my fortieth we splashed out and went to the Dominican Republic for two weeks. The all-inclusive resort was amazing, and the facilities, excursions and activities were so varied. There was scuba-diving training in the pool, quad biking on the beaches, all the usual water sports, an on-site trapeze training and show, rock climbing, on-site casino, and bars and restaurants.

Our first experience was the scuba training in the deep end of the pool. Leslie and I joined six others and got fully dressed up in all the scuba gear, including the weight belts and air tanks. We were told to put our masks on, just breathe normally, then sink to the bottom of the deep end and sit calmly in a circle with everyone else. The instructor then showed you how to use your regulator to help you float and how to put air bubbles in your mask to clear any water out. It really was a great feeling to sit on the bottom of the pool and just breathe normal air. Later in the week, we all went to the sea to do a real scuba-dive down to a sunken shipwreck, saw all the colourful tropical fish and fed them bananas! We even went out on a big boat and did the professional dive into the sea, where you sit on the side of the boat and fall backwards into the sea.

Our next experience was quad biking, which turned out to be a real adrenaline adventure. It was a baking hot thirty-degree day and we were just dressed in shorts and T-shirts, but were told to wear proper trainers and socks. The quads could seat two people, so I had Leslie on the back of mine, holding on tightly to me, and our son rode one on his own. We set off in a convoy of about eight quads along the road to start with, and then headed onto the beach. It was brilliant fun sliding everywhere and jumping over the sand dunes. I kept checking on Leslie and she said it was fun, and to keep going. The sea sprayed all over us as we drove along the edge of the shallow waves, but we didn't mind getting soaked because it cooled us down. Next on our trip was a jungle track with lots of twists, slopes and little jumps, which were easily tackled on our big quads. A quick fifteen-minute drinks break was followed by our final task of a dry river bed and an old dried-up waterfall. The river bed was really bumpy and rocky, but nothing compared to the old waterfall. We all stopped and looked up at the hillside and the monster, rocky, muddy slope rising up in front of us, and we all said, "No way! How the hell can you ride up that?"

Our guide just said, "Follow me; take the exact route I use, keep the throttle fully open – and DON'T stop!"

I was next in line and, after telling Leslie to hang on for grim death, I just went for it full speed and it worked like a dream: we just kept going up and up, until we reached the top. A few of the others struggled a bit, but we all made it up safely and clapped at our amazing achievement. On our return to the resort, we took our sunglasses off and all looked like pandas because of our sunburn and dusty faces.

My actual birthday arrived, and amongst other treats planned for my fortieth there was a big football match to go and watch. It was the World Cup qualifying match between Germany and England, played away in Germany. Unfortunately, the match wasn't being screened at the resort, so a large group of us had to get taxis into the local town and their main sports bar. This sports bar was just an amazing sight, with about a hundred football shirts from every nation hanging from the high ceilings, and with massive screens everywhere. At kick-off, the bar was rammed with rowdy English and German supporters, but it wasn't a good start when Germany scored an early goal. But, of course, as you probably remember, England went on to score five unanswered goals, with Michael Owen getting a hat-trick. WOW, what an atmosphere! The crowd was going mental and cheering, "We want six, we want six!" All the German supporters were shocked and just took all our jokes and chanting in good spirits. What a way to celebrate a birthday! Somehow, we staggered back to our resort in a fleet of taxis and all jumped in the pool to celebrate some more.

Of course, having a casino on site was just too tempting for my son and I! While my wife and friends would go to watch the evening shows, we would hit the tables and mainly play roulette. It was set up exactly like a proper casino, with the waitresses bringing drinks to us all night. It was brilliant fun, and although we weren't gambling big amounts, the tension was very real. At the end of one night, we had been very successful until we lost it all again, so in a last-ditch effort we gambled everything on Black – and it came in. Result! That was too stressful for me, but good to win.

CHAPTER 13

NIGHTCLUBS

Waiting on the rank outside the nightclubs was always entertaining and exhilarating, not knowing what was going to kick-off next. People getting thrown out by the bouncers was always eventful. I was number one on the rank, and keeping my fingers crossed for somebody sensible, when a fight started and the bouncers kicked a drunk out. He wouldn't give up, and ended up getting battered and covered in blood. He came up to my window and politely asked if he could get in. I said, "I think you would be better off getting an ambulance, mate!"

He pushed a £20 note through the window and begged me to take him home, so I agreed, as I felt sorry for him. When he got in, he apologised for the state of his clothes and said, "Did you see that? I was a right dickhead, wasn't I?" We laughed, and he said I was his hero for taking him home.

The respect you got from some people was very rewarding, and made up for all the arseholes we had to deal with. "Don't judge a book by its cover," as they say!

Another dramatic event was the night a bloke was so pissed off at the bouncers for being thrown out, he got in his BMW and drove it straight at them.

Thankfully, there were lots of three-foot metal posts in front of the nightclub, and the car ended up at forty-five degrees in the air, impaled on one of the posts. CHAOS! The bouncers ran over to the car, dragged him out and battered him before the police turned up. So, a few months later, I was just casually chatting to my passenger as we arrived at the leisure complex, and said, "Do you remember that prat who drove his BMW onto that post?"

He said, "Yes, that was ME!"

"OH, SHIT! That was you? Whoops!" Thankfully, he didn't mind my outburst, and just shrugged it off. That was a bit awkward.

The main taxi rank outside the nightclubs had spaces for about eight cars and then twenty-plus cars on the overflow rank opposite. All the drivers kept their doors locked so people couldn't just jump in at the back, and we always directed people to the very front car, as was the rule. Most people would come out in small groups and were easy to control, but on certain occasions at closing time, especially Christmas and New Year, there would be hundreds of people swarming around the rank, and it was like running the gauntlet when we drove into the pick-up area. To stop my car from being overrun by people, I would drive right past the crowd and stop further up, so the next people in line could run up to me, jump in and then we could quickly drive off safely away from the crowds. Another way to avoid the chaos was to pick up people off the side of the road where they had walked right up to the entrance to the complex, and were desperately waving £20 notes at us to make us stop.

I only saw it a couple of times, but when any of the cars on the rank feared for their safety, then we would all work together. Once, in the town on a quiet evening, there were about twelve of us all parked up, reading our papers, when a row started at the front of the queue. A group of drunks had turned violent and were threatening the first taxi with racist abuse because he wouldn't let them in his car. He was one of our many Asian drivers and a good friend. So we all got out of our cars and ganged up on this rowdy group of arseholes to protect our friend. We called the police, who were already on the way, because they had seen the trouble on the security cameras. But it got even worse when they started attacking and lashing out at the other cars on the rank, so we all had to run to our cars and drive away from the rank until the police had sorted it all out.

The other occasion was outside the nightclubs, when a mass brawl of about a hundred people came piling out of the club doors and started fighting with the bouncers.

Every single taxi had to quickly drive away together in a mass evacuation from the danger coming towards us. We all parked up at a safe distance away from the carnage and watched the police deal with the chaos. A few meat wagons later, everything was back to normal and we resumed our positions on the rank.

Because the nightclubs were so busy, they attracted all kinds of weirdos.

One normal-looking young bloke in a suit, whilst sitting in the front, started getting all his drugs and needles out, and said, "You don't mind if I shoot up, do you? I'll be done in a minute!"

What choice did I have? It was a bit late to stop, as I was driving fast up the dual carriageway, so I just carried on to the clubs. When we got there, I was not impressed at all and gave him a filthy look. He paid me and off he went.

Sometimes you just have to grit your teeth, be professional and carry on. When they've paid you, got out of the car and shut the door, then you can call them all the names under the sun as you drive away.

It never happened to me, but I have heard other drivers complain of this same situation. My nephew, who was a taxi driver at the same time as me, picked up two very attractive young women, who thought they would try to get a free ride by flirting and being sexy with him. He was a young father with a girlfriend at the time, and just wasn't interested in their antics. However, these girls were very persistent, and the girl in the front started grabbing at his dick. So he just stopped the car and let the meter run until she got the hint, paid him what she owed, and got out with the hump. I can understand how this situation sounds funny, but when you are stone-cold sober and are only doing your job to earn money, it gets a bit annoying when women try it on to get a freebie. It is also a very risky situation for a driver, because if he did decide to whip his dick out, the woman could quite easily turn on him and call him a pervert, report him, and he could be suspended. So, in other words, it's not worth the risk.

CHAPTER 14

ROAD RAGE

Road rage was always a problem. It seemed like, as soon as you put that taxi sign on top of your car, nearly every other car on the road had it in for you, or maybe it was just the bad standard of driving in the town. My car horn and middle finger were in constant use. It was essential to have a dash-cam fitted when they were available to buy. Many times my camera caught all sorts of dickheads and downright dangerous drivers doing stupid things in front of me. A few times when I got out of my car to confront someone, they said to me, "What are you going to do about it? You've got no proof!"

So I would just smile and say, "Think again, dickhead, you're on camera!" as I pointed towards my windscreen dash-cam, and they would back right down.

During our quiet times on the rank, we would entertain ourselves by laughing at each other's dash-cam footage. The worst incident I had was when I was driving through the town up to a mini roundabout to turn right; the car opposite me was going straight on, and was supposed to wait for me as I had right of way. Well, he had other ideas, and tried to go before I turned. He tooted ME, and gave me the wanker's sign.

So he got the middle finger back from me, as I turned right in front of him. When I looked in my mirror, all I could see was this car being driven as if a maniac was at the wheel. I had passengers on board, but they were oblivious to what was happening behind us. My fears came true, and we got stuck in traffic at the lights. Oh my God! The mad driver was five cars behind us, and he had jumped out of his car and was running up to us through the traffic. I locked all the doors and windows just before he got to us.

BANG, BANG on my window, swearing and cursing, trying to open my door, then he leant right across my windscreen, thumping with both fists. GREEN LIGHT, GO! I just floored it, and he fell off my bonnet and into the road. I made sure he didn't follow us by driving round in circles to get away from him. My passengers were in a state of shock, but thanked me for getting them home safely. We got away with it, but it was quite scary at the time.

Although not road rage, but taxi driver rage, a funny incident occurred when a taxi driver who was renting his taxi for about a year, had a very bad disagreement with the owner of the cab. The driver in question was a good friend of mine and worked part-time with us at our little supermarket taxi rank. One day, he turned up for work in a different taxi and explained about the problems he was having: he was so pissed off with the situation, he had done something rather stupid. Over the weekend, my friend had made a fifty-mile trip to another town, abandoned the car in the station car park, and got the train back here. So the owner of the cab had to pay someone to go and retrieve the car from the station car park! I was gobsmacked when he told me and didn't really believe him until it was confirmed a few days later by the really angry owner of the missing taxi. Although it was a silly thing to do, it was rather funny at the time.

When my son turned seventeen, his first and only thought was to pass his driving test. So he found an all-inclusive driving course which guaranteed a pass in ten days of intense driving. It was in Essex, so he went on the train and stayed in a B&B for ten nights. Previous to this, he had chosen a second-hand Vauxhall Corsa from a local garage, and I fitted it with a big stereo and sub-woofer he had bought for the car. Ten days later, he phoned us up to say he had passed first time and was on his way home. Well, everyone says not to drive too far on your first trip, but he drove all his mates to London as soon as he got back!

Nine months later, he got a court summons through the post, and had to tell me all about it. So, in another county somewhere, he had been on a fast dual carriageway and was egged on by his mates to try and get 100mph out of his 1000cc Corsa.

Luckily for him, he only managed 99mph, because he was being tailed by a traffic police car which had speed equipment on board, and he was pulled over by them. They weren't impressed with his speeding, but were surprised that he got 99mph out of a 1-litre Corsa.

His court day arrived and he had a solicitor there to help him keep his licence, as you only get six points' allowance in the first year of driving. The judge took into consideration that it was his first offence, and he wasn't driving in a dangerous manner, so gave him five points and a £250 fine. Very close to a ban, and it served as a strong warning.

Six years later, he splashed out big time on a Ford Focus ST, a favourite car of mine as well, and he even let me drive it to town when I dropped them off for a night out. Silly boy, letting me loose in a car like that with a top speed of 150mph!

CHAPTER 15

SCARY AND FUN

We've all heard of 'Sods Law' or 'Murphy's Law'. Well, my typical moment happened on the very day that I had my vasectomy. At the grand old age of thirty-three, I had to man up and get the snip to prevent my wife from getting pregnant, as she had an illness which was dangerous if she got pregnant again. So I booked into a private clinic to jump the NHS queue, and was successfully snipped on a Monday morning. I got a taxi there and back because you were specifically told before the operation that you cannot drive for twenty-four hours afterwards because your balls swell up to the size of melons. I got home and put my feet up for the rest of the morning with some frozen peas on my swollen balls. In the afternoon, my wife got a very strange phone call from my Mum, mumbling and crying, and it sounded like she was in shock. Ten minutes later, my mum phoned back and said, "Dad has had a heart attack; he's alive and I'm going to the hospital with him in the ambulance!"

Damn! The only time I was not allowed to drive, and my Dad had a bloody heart attack! My wife couldn't drive, so she had to get a taxi to the hospital in the next town. The next evening, I could drive again, so we all went to visit my Dad properly in my car. Luckily, he survived and went on to live another twenty years. During those last twenty years my dad carried on with his big passion for cycling and would regularly cycle more than one hundred miles in a day! In the last few years of this period though his damaged heart was starting to fail and cause low blood pressure, which gave him blackouts and one day he woke up in a hedge at the side of a road and had to give up on his beloved cycling for good!

One of the scariest things that can happen to you as a taxi driver is when the police pull you over with their blue lights on, and tell you to follow them to an undisclosed location. They picked drivers at random and with no warning, and then they lead you to the underground Town Hall car park, where the Taxi Inspectors were waiting with the MOT inspectors, the council benefits team and document checkers. You waited nervously while they did all their checks and asked you, "How many hours do you work, how much do you earn, are you claiming any benefits, and do you have another job?"

To which I replied, "I work forty hours a week, and I have an accountant, so you'll have to speak to him about that!"

Thankfully, everything was in order, and my tyres were all legal. This could have been very bad because each bald tyre was three points on your licence. Quite a few cars were taken off the road for various offences, and a couple had their taxi licences suspended pending investigations. It was good in a way because the bad drivers got caught out and were punished. The night shift that night was great because all the other drivers had gone home and we cleaned up with a busy night.

A few years later, I was warned by a driver who had been pulled over earlier in the day, so I went straight home after my day shift to avoid all that shit happening again.

Another time, one of my regulars approached my car to get in. Now normally he was very polite and unassuming; he got into trouble a lot, but could handle his drink, and was no problem. BUT TODAY was very different. He got in, and off we went. I could see he was very angry and wound up over something, and then I realised that he had a KNIFE in each hand, and started to rub them together to sharpen them! He raged, "I am going to KILL HIM, I am going to KILL HIM! That dirty son of a bitch is going to DIE!" He said who he was after, and I understood that it was one of the town's villains. I dropped him off at a pub and got out of the way rather quickly! A few weeks later, I saw the very same villain walking down the high street as bold as brass, so I assumed that my knife-wielding passenger had either bottled it after having second thoughts, or couldn't find who he was looking for at the time!

In twenty years on nights and nine years on days, I was never threatened or assaulted, apart from just the one time when I was punched in the face by a gypsy. So, I picked up one girl from the nightclubs; she got in the front, and asked if we could pick up her friends that had started walking. No problem with that, so off we went. We travelled down the dual carriageway to find her group of friends, but when I stopped, I realised there were four of them, AND they were all gypsies. They all got in, but angrily I said, "I am not taking you to the site. There are five of you in total, and I'm going nowhere. I want you ALL to get out, otherwise I will drive straight back to the club, and the police will get you out!"

As I did a U-turn and stopped, they all got out and the last one punched me in the face from the back seat! I felt relieved that they were out of my car, but obviously really pissed off about the punch; so, as soon as I got back to the nightclub, I spoke to the police and they roared off with their sirens and blue lights on to try and catch up with them, to arrest them for assaulting me. They never got back to me, so I assumed they couldn't find them. Even though I got punched, it felt good that I had stood up to them, made my point and they had backed down.

As a trusted taxi driver, you got used to being an 'Agony Aunt' and a 'Confidant'. People would tell us all about their secrets, medical problems, relationship or marital issues, also all the 'lads' banter' and the girls' 'gossip' or 'bitching'. After years of listening to everyone, the more knowledge you picked up, the more you could give out sound advice to people. The fun of it was that you could latch on to each conversation, be part of it, and put across your points of view. I had a great sense of humour, and jokes were always dirty and full of innuendo. If you could be your passengers' best friend for their journey, then you would get good tips and hopefully no trouble. When I first started out I was not very street wise, a bit shy and naive so it was quite an education learning about all sorts of fun sexual terms and phrases, positions, rhyming slang and people's personal intimate experiments and accidents! One bloke told me once that during a very aggressive shagging session he actually ripped his "banjo string!", DAMN! That must have been painful! (that is the piece of skin under the head of your penis that is attached to you foreskin!) Wow! Then there were several confessions of anal toys getting stuck and needing a hospital trip to remove! I learnt what a "pearl necklace" and a "Mexican pancake" were, also the terms "missionary, cow girl, DP, BJ, S&M, doggy style, and 69!" Two blokes confessed to me that they had taken a short-cut across a farmer's field, only to realise that there was a bloody scary bull waiting for them! As they ran for the safety of the fence one of them struggled to get over the barbed wire on top and ripped his ball sack so badly he had to call an ambulance to get stitched up! OUCH!

One of my great guilty pleasures over the years was poking fun at the couples and their drunk partners, and it was normally the women who were guilty of this. It was sometimes the staggering difference between being SOBER and BLIND DRUNK. So, when I arrived at my pick-up point, the husband or boyfriend would say, "I'm so sorry, Adrian, but she's had too much to drink, but she definitely won't be sick!"

I giggled when she collapsed in the front seat, blabbering some nonsense about, "I'm never doing this again, this is so embarrassing!"

One even said to me, "The ladies was too busy, so I went round the back of the pub, and as I was peeing on some bin liners, they suddenly all moved, and a tramp said, 'Excuse me, do you mind? I was sleeping there'!" I hadn't laughed so much in years!

I usually said to the partner, "Ha, ha, you can't take them anywhere these days, can you? I'm going to have a field day with her when I next pick her up and she's sober!"

When I did get a chance to wind them up when they were sober, it would be, "Don't you remember running around that field half-naked, chasing that cow?" or "Don't you remember squatting in that hedge over there to have a pee?" or "Don't you remember swinging round that lamp post, singing your head off?" Good banter and laughs. Well, they gave me loads of ammunition, so it would have been criminal not to!

Our town taxi rank was positioned in the pedestrian zone and was strictly 'Taxis Only'; but some drivers thought they were clever and tried parking on our rank to go into McDonald's to get their takeaway. BIG MISTAKE! If there was a private car parked on our rank, then we would just all park really close to it, or double rank next to it if the rank was full, and just walk off to have a group chat. The driver of the offending car would do their nut when they couldn't get out. As there were no drivers in the taxis around them, we just shrugged our shoulders and told them they were idiots for parking there. They would start to get very angry and threaten to phone the police. So we told them to go ahead and do just that, because they would then get a ticket for parking on the rank. When we all moved up the rank and finally let them out, they would rev their engines and wheel-spin away, but we just waved at them and laughed, because they were idiots.

CHAPTER 16

SOCIAL LIVES

Before I was married, my social life was a bit quiet, because I was heavily into cycle road racing and time trials, but my friends would always get me to go to Trafalgar Square in London for New Year's Eve. So, one year, we got the train into Euston station and started walking from there. On the way we did a pub crawl, and because all of us had cans of beer in plastic bags, we would hide these outside before we went into the pub. The last pub we visited had scaffolding outside, which was a great place to hide our bags. When we came out to get our bags, somebody else had left theirs as well, so we pinched the whole lot and did a runner through the crowds. When we had stopped laughing, we saw a fire engine coming slowly down the road. Some people had already climbed on to it, so we all jumped on as well! We were ringing the bell and messing about with the flood lights, having a brilliant time. They were on their way to Trafalgar Square, so we got a lift all the way there. It got to five minutes to midnight, and we were all dancing in the fountain, trying to get in front of the television cameras, when our mate slipped over and knocked himself out. He woke up at ten minutes past midnight in the back of an ambulance and missed all the fun. About one a.m., we all headed to Soho and crashed in the all-night sex cinemas and then got the eight a.m. train home from Euston. Epic night!

It wasn't all work and no play; we did have social lives and the occasional taxi drivers' night out. As an avid Arsenal fan, if it was quiet out and about, then I would sneak off to the snooker club to have a couple of drinks with my taxi mates, watch the footy and have a few games of snooker. When it got to eleven o'clock, my phone would start ringing and then I would shoot off to do all my bookings. Most of our lads' nights out were usually just football, tenpin bowling or pub and a curry. One night, we were all told to dress smart as we were going to London on the train for a pub crawl. So we all ended up in the pubs in Shoreditch, having a merry time. At the end of the night, we all followed our 'leader' down the street and he got us all into the lap dancing club. Well, there's a first time for everything, and we certainly enjoyed ourselves. I can see why it's very easy to spend a lot of money on the dancers. After our brilliant night out, we got the last train back from Euston; but, of course, being so pissed, we missed our stop and had to get taxis back from the next town. Needless to say, our antics had to remain secret from our wives, ha, ha!

Having been to the Emirates football stadium for the guided tour, my son had promised us tickets to see a match there, and two months later, he came up trumps with tickets to see Arsenal *v* Norwich on the Saturday. Wicked! So we got to the stadium by train and tube and stopped off at the Famous Cock Tavern for a few pre-match drinks and lots of

Arsenal banter and laughs with all the regular fans. As the crowds grew, we just followed everyone else through the streets until we reached the stadium.

We had plenty of time to take all the selfies we needed in front of the entrance, and then found our seats under the huge jumbo screen near the away supporters' section. The game finished 4-1 to Arsenal, and there was just an amazing celebration every time we scored a goal. After the match, it was back to the pub again for more fun, banter and drinks, and even on the tube back to Euston all the fans were full of laughter and songs. Just an amazing day out, and we couldn't wait to watch the highlights on *Match of the Day* to see all the goals properly and see if we could pick ourselves out of the crowd!

Of course, my son had many nights out, and every weekend would end up phoning me at three a.m. after the nightclubs finished for a lift home. I didn't mind at all, because I was out working anyway, and, of course, I knew he was getting home safe if I picked him up.

A few months ago, me, my son and his best mate were having a few drinks and they were telling me about all the wild Ibiza-style lads' holidays they had been on, and all the stupid pranks they pulled on each other. The best one, which was hysterical, started with a simple bottle of sun tan oil that one of them was using every day. So, after using this bottle, the other lads would pee into it and mix it up. The next day, the same thing happened, with more pee. Eventually, after constant use, he would start to notice the urine smell and began to comment on the stink around their pool area. He kept using the oil, and all his mates would just smile at him, until one day he clocked what had been going on. He was livid and threw the bottle of oil at all his laughing mates. When it all calmed down, a young girl walked past and asked if she could use some of the oil. With a devilish grin, he said, "Sure, love, take the whole bottle if you like!" So she gleefully laid down and covered herself in this piss oil, and the whole swimming area erupted in laughter!

The Millennium new year was fast approaching, and all the drivers were saying how amazing it was going to be, and how they were going to charge triple-time and everyone would be out partying. But the feeling I got from talking to my passengers about it was that everybody was scared of the 'Millennium Bug' and didn't want to go anywhere because of the computer bug that might cause chaos everywhere. Many years ago, my dad had told me about the computer problem that was going to happen with all the old programs as we went into the year 2000. He was a computer operations manager, and he said it was because the lazy computer programmers had always started the year date with '19' back in the eighties and just assumed that everything would be upgraded before 2000.

I made my mind up to have a big house party, and I invited all my regulars, family and friends to come round for the big New Year's Eve event. We were expecting a lot of people to come, so there was tons of food and drink, and all downstairs and the conservatory were decorated with balloons and party poppers. Unfortunately, none of my regulars turned up, but there were still plenty of us to have an amazing party. My video camera got plenty of use, and still today we watch it back, and admire all the great drunken dancing and antics. My favourite drunken dance was by Leslie and Aimee who did a fantastic routine from the film *The Full Monty*, where they danced in a line to Tom Jones singing "You can leave your hat on"! Just so poignant now.

A few days into the new year and all the drivers were saying what a crap night the New Year's Eve had been because nobody had left their houses!

CHAPTER 17

SUPERMARKET FUN AND GAMES

So after nineteen years of night shifts I was finally in a position to change to day shifts on the taxi rank in the town, but still do Friday and Saturday nights to keep my regulars going until I finally packed in nights for good! After a few months my old boss Alf spoke to me on the rank and asked if I was interested in working at the local Asda store part-time, taking all the customers home with their shopping which we would load and unload for them as part of the service. It was like a little gold mine because the main town rank was too far away from the shop on the top of a hill, so our little rank outside the store was extremely busy! I did this part-time for a year and then Alan, one of the full-time drivers, moved away so I was next in line to go full-time! I eagerly took up the offer and joined the other drivers, Alf, Colin, Peter, John, Pete, and later Derek, Chris, Bill, Pete M, Andy, Justin, Paul and Mark. Over the ten years that I worked at Asda I made loads of friends with all the customers, staff, management and drivers, just too many to mention, but they will all remember me!

I was waiting for some shoppers outside a supermarket exit door, when in my mirror I saw a car reverse up to the entrance door, open its big boot, and a group of gypsies wheeled out two big trollies rammed with stolen food and drink, upended them straight into the boot, and drove off in seconds. Everyone was just standing there open-mouthed in disbelief at what had just happened. This sort of thing went on, and they just got away with it because they drove straight up to their caravan site and disappeared. Another time, at the very same supermarket, I was working with my old boss 'ALF', who had the contract for working outside the shop. We were just standing next to the exit door chatting, when out ran a shoplifter carrying bottles of alcohol.

My boss managed to trip him up, and the thief dropped all the bottles of booze. The police had been called, but in the meantime we both had to SIT on the shoplifter until they arrived to arrest him officially. So, one woman police officer turned up to arrest him, and as she tried to put the handcuffs on him, he spun round and tried to PUNCH HER! My old boss put his martial arts to good use again, and the thief was soon sprawled on the floor and in 'cuffs. Reinforcements arrived and the male officers didn't take very kindly to him trying to hit their female colleague. I wouldn't want to have been in his shoes when they took him away in the meat wagon.

Supermarket pick-up again; this time I was taking a blind lady home with a lot of shopping in the boot. It was raining heavily as we approached her house in a cul-de-sac. I hit a big puddle and splashed a man walking on the path. Oops! As I stopped at her house, he came running up to the car and started going mental at me. I think he was on drugs or something, but I knew I had to get out of my car to help the blind woman to her door, as well as her shopping. The druggie was in my face the whole time; it was a nightmare. I was soaked, so I just screamed at the guy, "If you're going to hit me, then you do know you can go to prison for hitting a taxi driver?" Thankfully, it worked, and he backed down and staggered off. The poor old blind lady didn't realise what was going on, what with all the shouting and everything, so when I explained, she invited me in for a cup of tea and cake to thank me.

It was a quiet day outside the supermarket, and I was parked right next to the busy cashpoint in the late afternoon, when suddenly a woman started shouting, "Oh my God!" at the cashpoint.

We all went over to investigate, and discovered that the whole front of the cashpoint was loose, and was actually FAKE. Someone was using this sophisticated set-up to clone people's cards and get their PIN numbers. We suspected a man at the back of the car park, who had been sitting in his Mercedes all day on his laptop. The police arrived quietly and blocked him in to arrest him for questioning. We were told later that it was an organised crime gang from Eastern Europe operating over here.

Handling customers' shopping was always interesting, especially when spillages and breakages happened. Every now and then, something would fall and break on the ground, like jars of pasta sauce, pickled onions, beetroot, gherkins, wines and spirits, most of which would splash onto my shoes, jeans or bare legs. The most common leakage was from the plastic containers of milk that split and leaked in the boot while we were driving to their house. When we picked up the carrier bag from the boot, it would have leaked everywhere; and, of course, I would have to clean up the mess straight away before it started to stink. To help combat this problem, we all bought tough plastic boot trays that would catch all the leaks and could easily be lifted out and washed.

So I had been working on our little taxi rank outside the supermarket for about a year now, and today was 1st September, and it was my birthday. I was in a great mood, as the sun was shining and we were quite busy. Customers were waiting patiently with their full shopping trolleys to be loaded into our boots. I pulled into our pick-up area, but there was a car parked right in the way, so I gave him a quick toot on my horn and politely asked him to move out of the way so I could get to the trolley to load up. He didn't move, so I got out of my car and approached his open window to ask him to move. Well, the ignorant git decided to get funny with me: he got all up in my face and started threatening me. The argument got rather heated, and he tried to punch me. I had to defend myself by pushing him in the chest with both hands. At this point, he fell to the ground and pretended that he was hurt, claiming that I had actually punched HIM. He then started shouting, "He assaulted me. I want this driver sacked!"

The manager and security guard came rushing out to separate us, and after giving the police a statement, I had to go home and cool down, and was not allowed to work at the store until the matter had been resolved. Thankfully, the lady I was trying to pick up at the time had seen the whole incident and gave a full statement. One week later, I was interviewed under caution and taped by the Taxi Inspectors at the Town Hall. I felt like a bloody criminal! They could tell I was angry, and I told them the accuser was a bloody idiot who had hit me first and I had to hit him back in self-defence. This was backed up by my lady witness, whose statement said the same thing. I was reinstated back at the shop and the idiot was banned from the supermarket.

We had our fair share of taxi wars in the town, and one that had been brewing for a long time at our little taxi rank outside the supermarket in the town was caused by jealousy over our contract that my old boss 'ALF' had with the management there, who only wanted us six full-time drivers to be there, because of the excellent customer service we provided, which included helping load everyone's shopping into the boot, and to their door at the destination. All the drivers had to pay a weekly rent to work outside the store, and this in turn was paid to the biggest taxi company in the town who, many years before, had sub-contracted it out to 'ALF'. Everyone was happy with this arrangement until the big taxi company got a new boss, and he got greedy. One day, this new boss came to the store in his fancy car and proceeded to have a big slanging match outside with 'ALF'. I witnessed it all and it got so bad that we had to call the police. The following day, 'ALF' was nowhere to be seen and his phone was switched off. Eventually, we got a distressed phone call from his wife saying that the police had come banging on their door at five thirty a.m. and dragged him down the police station for questioning. Later that afternoon, about five p.m., 'ALF' turned up looking tired and pissed off. He said, "Do you know what that bastard did? He only accused me of racially abusing him and threatening to beat him up with a baseball bat! They treated me like a criminal and kept me in the cells all day!"

Anyone who witnessed the argument, including me, gave our statements to the police, and all the charges were dropped. I think the police must have had very strong words with this big company boss (arsehole!) about false accusations and wasting police time, because it all blew over after that. About a year later, this big boss went bankrupt and in later years left the country altogether.

CHAPTER 18

ACCIDENTS

As a family, we went on some great holidays abroad. Having been to Walt Disney World, Florida, one summer, we decided to go again, but this time at Christmas for three weeks in 2001. Of course, we all know the terrible events that happened on 11th September that year, and so we then had to decide, do we cancel or still go? We decided to go, and it was a brilliant holiday. The night before we left for the airport, I worked a few hours in the evening. I saw people waiting at the train station, and turned right to enter the station, when BANG! My passenger window was smashed to pieces! I got out and examined my car for more damage and then I realised what had happened. I could see a motorbike lying in the road, and its rider unconscious next to it. OH, SHIT! He must have been speeding or had no lights on his bike or something. Luckily, the police let me drive my car home, as I had explained about flying out on holiday the next morning. While we were on holiday, my brother-in-law sorted all the insurance out, and as the car was a write-off, he even found me another car to buy on our return.

The car I went to look at with my brother-in-law was a Ford Granada 2.9-litre, 24-valve. The man selling it had numerous young lads after it because it had a COSWORTH engine and was a very fast car, but none of them could afford the insurance on it. This was no problem for me, because Hackney Carriage Public Hire insurance was the same whatever car I had. £1200 and three days later, I was back on the road again. After a few days of driving my new car, I decided to give it a bit of stick down a quiet road. It was an automatic and had a kick-down feature to it, so when you put your foot flat to the floor, it would drop down a gear and accelerate extremely quickly. Oh my God, it sounded like a racing engine and revved beautifully! I thought, *Damn, I've got to see how fast this thing will go on the bypass!* My opportunity came a few weeks later when I went to Watford to pick up my wife and friends after their shopping trip. As soon as I got onto the beginning of the A41 bypass, I floored it and didn't let off. We were doing 100mph at the top of the rise, and as we went downhill into the valley, it quickly rose to 130, 140, but then I ran out of road because our turning was coming up, but it would have gone faster for sure. Even at those speeds, the car handled brilliantly and felt safe, because it was built to go that fast. I didn't tell anyone how fast we had gone until we got home, so I got away with it, and never attempted it again. Of course, 100mph and above is an instant ban, and I wasn't going to risk my licence again.

Six months later, after my accident with the motorbike, I was charged with 'driving without due care and attention'.

As I was convinced that I was innocent of this charge, I took it to court and defended myself to avoid £1000 in solicitor's fees. A week before the court date, I worked on my statement and questions I needed to ask in court. My brother-in-law came with me for moral support and watched from the gallery. Defending yourself is very interesting and nerve-racking at the same time, but as I got into my stride, I became more confident at speaking. Once I had defended myself from their solicitor, I was then allowed to cross examine all the witnesses and the police officers who were present at the accident. I managed to prove the motorbike was speeding, but apparently the lights were all functioning properly, and so I should have seen him in time to stop. The judge was actually quite impressed with my performance, and felt a bit sorry for me. Thankfully, the rider of the bike wasn't badly injured, so I just got six points and a small fine.

CHAPTER 19

11th SEPTEMBER

We all remember where we were on 11th September, and watching it unfold on television, like some crazy disaster movie, it didn't seem real, and we were talking about nothing else for weeks after. Exactly one week after the twin towers collapsed and killed almost three thousand people, my mood was still sombre, but when I pulled onto the back of the rank and walked up to chat to the other drivers, they were all laughing and joking with huge excitement. "Did you hear? Have you heard? It's amazing! Five of the drivers in a lottery syndicate WON 6 MILLION POUNDS last night, as it was a roll-over, so they get 1.2 MILLION POUNDS EACH!"

One of the winners was a good friend of mine, and only in his thirties, so he was set up for life now, I guessed. A week later, when the winners had resurfaced after the shock, we all went out for drinks, and quizzed them about their feelings and future plans. My mate said, "I was working Saturday night when my wife rang me to tell me she had triple-checked the winning numbers. I was just picking up a customer and could barely drive the car because of my excitement. I just said to my customer,

'Don't pay me; it's free!' Ha, ha!" He said that he had got lots of begging phone calls, and they were upset and crying because the pressure of it all was getting to them. We all gave them lots of sound advice, and that's what mates do. My mate carried on working part-time, as he said it kept him out of the pub! He bought a lovely big house and invested the rest for his retirement.

CHAPTER 20

BUNCEFIELD

Saturday 10th December 2005 was the usual busy night, with it getting near to Christmas. I got home at three a.m. and went to bed as usual. Three hours later, I was rudely awoken by a THUD! THUD! THUD! It was like someone falling down the stairs.

My wife was awake next to me, so it wasn't the stairs. I looked out of the window and I knew immediately that there was something very wrong, because everybody was out in the street in their dressing gowns and it was freezing cold as well. I quickly shoved some clothes on and ran outside. To my horror, I could now see what everybody was staring at. In the direction of the Buncefield oil depot and storage facility, only half a mile from us, behind the industrial estate, was the HUGE orange and yellow glow of a massive fire. Our first thoughts were that it could have been a plane crash, because everyone had always said, "If Buncefield ever blows up, we won't survive the explosion."

A few of us walked down to the industrial estate to get a closer look, but were stopped by evacuating oil depot workers, who told us it was an accidental explosion and the fumes could be very harmful, so it was best to stay indoors.

Then I got a phone call from my Dad, who lived five miles away and had heard the explosion. He said it was now on the telly.

Sunday was my day off, so we just sat watching all the coverage on the news, trying to work out how we all survived the blast. I later found out that our house was protected by the hillside next to the industrial valley, and so the explosive blast had travelled up the hill and OVER our housing estate. The estates either side, IN the valley, got the full force of the blast and had ALL their windows blown out and other damage to cars and buildings.

Amazingly, nobody was killed. It was SO fortunate that it happened on a Sunday morning, because if it had been a week day, then I think hundreds could have been killed. When you saw the pictures of the devastation, it looked like a nuclear bomb had been dropped on the site. Half of the industrial estate had to be demolished and rebuilt. For the next few weeks driving around the town, all you could see was the MASSIVE black plume of smoke billowing up for miles, and we wondered if it was ever going to be put out. When I drove to one area of the town, on the hillside overlooking the industrial site, all you could see were dozens of TV vans parked up, with all their film crews and journalists doing their live broadcasts and interviews. One of my regulars was a fireman, and he was working twelve-hour shifts for weeks at the site, and every time I picked him up, he would give me all the updates. Lots of residents had to live in hotels for months until their homes were safe to live in again because of the structural damage to their homes.

CHAPTER 21

CHARACTERS

Over the years we had many regulars who were real characters. One was a window cleaner, and a giant of a man, a bit like 'Hagrid' without the beard! We would always see him strolling around the estates carrying his ladders on his shoulder, wearing the SAME old clothes EVERY DAY. So by now I was working days with my old boss 'ALF' and three other drivers outside a supermarket in the town. Our window cleaner giant did his shopping here, and when you saw him next in line to be picked up, your heart sank, because he STANK like an old chamois leather! Not only that, but you feared for the suspension on the car when he squeezed in the front seat. In fact, not long after buying a very new Mondeo, which still had the manufacturer's warranty on it, Hagrid got in the front seat and after adjusting himself, actually managed to break the seat! He had seized the back of the seat and it wouldn't tilt backwards or forwards when he got out. Obviously, he was very apologetic, and said he would pay for it to be fixed. I went to my local Ford main dealer, from where the car had been bought, and luckily they said the whole seat could be replaced under warranty. Result! Instead of the usual-sized shopping bags, he liked to shove all his shopping into a massive laundry bag that would take two of us to lift into the boot, and again when we got to his house. We were always polite to him, and he was also a very good tipper. His main interest and hobby was chess, and he had worked his way up to 'Grandmaster' level on his computer. All our conversations were about chess, which was very amusing, but he did know a lot of jokes, which kept us entertained. I always kept a can of air freshener in the boot ready to fumigate the car once he was indoors, and I had a ten-minute drive back to the store with all the windows open, but the PONG would always linger.

Another day, I stopped at our little supermarket rank to pick up the next customer, and as I was loading the shopping in the boot, I noticed the local tramp sitting on the bench where customers wait for us. I carried on with my fare and when I got back he was still sitting there, and the other customers were just going around him to get in their taxis. When it was quiet, I asked one of the staff about the tramp, and they said he wanted a cab but no one would take him. *Oh, damn! I'm going to have to take one for the team here, just to get him out of the way!* So I asked him if he had any money, which he did. So I wound down all my windows and asked him for directions. As he got in, I realised my big mistake straight away. He looked like he'd never washed in his life, his clothes looked like something off a scarecrow, and he literally stank of shit. All I could do was hold my breath, bite my tongue and take him home. He paid me and thanked me, and off he waddled down the road.

I stopped the car around the next corner as I thought I was going to puke. Then I thought, *How the hell can you get into that kind of state?* Never again! I fumigated the car so it smelt sweet again and told nobody else about it.

One stand-out character in the town that everybody knew, but were quite intimidated by, was a tall, bald, old man who was covered head to toe in tattoos and piercings. He wore black leather bondage-type gear and even his face and head were covered in tattoos and loads of piercings. He would always be seen walking up and down the high street with his bags of shopping, and stopped to talk to people about his life and previous job as a bank manager.

A supermarket regular got into my car one day and said to me, "Hi, Adrian, you know where I live, don't you? Well, you will be in for a shock when we get there, because the police are at my next-door neighbour's house taking away all the CANNABIS plants that he was growing in his loft!"

So the police had caught this family out by using a police helicopter fitted with thermal imaging equipment, and it had hovered over the houses to detect all the extra heat in people's lofts generated by the strong lamps used. We got to this woman's house and the police were carrying out all the plants and equipment used by her neighbours. I knew for sure that they must have found more houses on this council estate by the same method.

A lovely lady who became a special friend of mine and Aimee's was Michele, who apart from being a regular customer of ours at Asda, was Aimee's work colleague and friend. Whenever I picked up Michele from Asda we would always have a good laugh and great chats about everything, including all her work prizes she won for hitting her sales targets! Michele moved away many years ago but all of us have remained in contact all the time and support each other when needed as lifelong friends.

Picking up all the 'yummy mummies' was always fun; but, of course, we were always very professional and true gentlemen! One woman in particular always stood out because she was about fifty but had the body of a twenty-year-old. I'm sure she did it on purpose, because she always wore tight skinny jeans and sat in the front with us, and had such a dirty sense of humour. The worst of it was that when we got to her house and walked behind her with her shopping, you couldn't help but admire her perfect arse in those tight jeans. Just awful; I don't know how I coped. Ha, ha!

Waiting outside the supermarket in the hot summer months was very tiring in the heat, because the store was built on a hill and had little shade during the day, so it was like sitting on top of someone's roof. We would either lock our cars and wait inside where the air conditioning was on, or sit in our cars with our own air conditioning on. It was so nice driving around all day in a cold car that I didn't want to go home for lunch and get out of the car! Occasionally, it would get up to a hundred degrees. All our passengers just loved getting into our cold cars when it was so hot outside. This was all fine until the air conditioning broke down on the car, which happened to me a few times and was absolutely horrible when you had to open all your windows and let all the hot air in, and then start sweating. Working in the heat was always tiring, and we would be shattered when we got home. It made such a difference when I was in my cold car all day, and I would be chilled out and relaxed at the end of the day.

Over the years working on the taxi ranks, you made a lot of good friends with all the other drivers. We would all get together for chats and a laugh about various incidents that had happened to us. We all looked out for each other on the road, and it was an unwritten law that you always let another driver out of a junction. There were lots of drivers with extrovert characters, and one such driver was in his late forties, very tall, but not really overweight as such, and he loved his golf. In fact, he was a scratch player, and could have been a professional. He was very chatty and knowledgeable and always gave advice to anyone who would listen, especially about golf. One of his main earners was a school run contract, and to do these reliably, every driver always had a back-up driver to call on if needed. One morning his back-up driver got a devastating phone call from the driver's wife, saying that she had just found him slumped in his chair in the front room, having DIED from a massive heart attack. Everyone on the rank was in shock and desperately sad for his wife and child that were now left alone. Three weeks later, we took it in shifts to take flowers to the house, go to the funeral and wake, and to give him the best send-off from all of us.

Opposite the front of the taxi rank in the town is a multi-storey car park, and occasionally, while queuing on the rank, there would suddenly be a flurry of police activity, and all the roads around the roundabout would be blocked off. It was then that we realised there was a man standing at the top of the car park, threatening to jump off. Back then, twenty-five years ago, we all laughed it off and just thought they were attention-seeking idiots. But in the last few years everybody is now much more aware of people's mental health issues and how it is very important to talk to friends and family about ANY troubles or issues, because there is ALWAYS a solution or answer to anything that life throws at us. Money issues, family or marriage problems can all be resolved just by talking to someone who is prepared to listen, not pass judgement, and offer sound advice. Talk is cheap, but could save a life.

Many times, of course, I would pick up all sorts of older passengers in their eighties and nineties who would tell me some really amazing stories about their interesting lives and many war stories. As Albert in "Only fools and horses" would say, "During the war.....!" Ha ha! I was fascinated by all the war stories and just how young they had all been to do such important jobs! One old boy confided in me that he had been the captain of a submarine at the grand old age of twenty-five, was the eldest of the crew who were aged between eighteen and twenty! Their submarine would regularly have to pass through mine-fields and it would be a nerve shredding, hot and sweaty deathly silence as they all held their breath and preyed as they silently and slowly inched their way through the deadly mine-fields! Then occasionally passing war ships would drop depth charges and they would have to dive very quickly and wait silently for the all-clear! To go through all that at such a young age must have been so terrifying for all of them and I was just gobsmacked that he had survived all that and was sat next to me at the age of eighty-five telling his fascinating story!

Ah, my lovely teenage daughter and her friends: very interesting memories! So, one Saturday night after a long shift, I got a message over the radio to go into the office straight away. It was three a.m. by then, and the radio operator told me, "I've just had a phone call from Milton Keynes police station. Can you go and pick up your daughter, as she was caught with her friends riding on the trains without tickets?"

So, after a very angry drive up to Milton Keynes, the police told me she had been let off with a caution and that she was very lucky to be found by the police because there was a rapist on the loose. Being only fifteen at the time, it was very worrying for all concerned. As you can imagine, the trip back home was very tense. I didn't say a word to her the whole way. She could see I had steam coming out of my ears! Hopefully, a lesson learned for her.

Our son is six years younger than my daughter, and growing up he always had a funny dressing-up thing going on with his school friends and mates, with costumes and make-up. We needn't have worried, though, as he soon started having regular girlfriends. Drinking, parties and wild holidays were his thing, but also the crazy fancy dress COSTUMES. When he was nineteen, he moved out to a shared rental house with three of his best mates, and they had a wild moving-in party. Of course, it all ended badly, and a fight started with another group of gate-crashing idiots, so he had to call the police to calm it all down. When the police knocked on his door, he rather embarrassingly opened it to reveal he was wearing a FAT FAIRY suit! The police had a good laugh about it, but did arrest the troublemakers for him.

CHAPTER 22

FREE MONEY AND TIPS

It was just a normal day, waiting to pick up my next fare at the supermarket, when my next customer got in and said, "Well, that was a result! I just went to get £10 out of the cash machine over there, and it gave me a £20 note by mistake. I checked my balance and it only stated £10 as going out."

I quickly jumped out of the car and ran over to the cashpoint to try this for myself, and the same thing happened: £20 instead of £10. Holy shit, the security guys must have messed up big time when they loaded the machine up in the morning. I quickly took my passengers home and raced back to the store, got out all my credit and bank cards and started banging away at the cashpoint. I was at it on and off all day until I had reached the limit on all my cards. By the time I had gone home in the evening, I had accumulated about £500 in free cash. By now, word had got around, and a queue had formed. People were taking it in turns to have three goes at it each. It was a lovely summer's evening, and everybody was excited, laughing and joking about how long it was going to last. Eventually, the inevitable happened: the machine went out of service and the bonanza was over, so we all went home. In the following weeks, we all wondered if the banks would want the money back, but nothing ever happened and we got away with it.

As everyone knows, tipping a taxi driver is all part of our culture and is very much appreciated by all drivers for the valuable service they provide. I was very fortunate to work in the cash-only era, and apart from the income tax benefits (hiding cash under the mattress syndrome!), another lucrative earner came in the form of the introduction of the one- and two-pound coins, a gift from heaven. So, imagine everyone's loose pockets full of pound coins and change from all the rounds of drinks. Our back seats were like collection trays for all the coins. After every fare, all of us savvy drivers would always check the back seats and footwells for coins, and about once a week pull up the back seat completely to reveal a goldmine of coins.

The front seats were also good for money loss. If you were lucky, when hoovering the car out you would occasionally find some folded notes. One time I found £100 in twenties by the front passenger door sill, which could easily have fallen out or been seen by the next passenger. My cash box was always an old Vitalite tub, which I hid under my car mat out of sight. Looking back, it was always a big risk having up to £200 hidden in my wallet in my driver's door, but in twenty-nine years I was thankfully never threatened with being robbed.

Every now and then we would be warned on the grapevine, or by the police, about fake £20 notes circulating. I came across a few myself, but thankfully they were easy to spot by feel of the paper and poor or no watermarks. We always confiscated any we were given and handed them into the police.

My daughter just read this story and confessed to me that when she was a teenager and I was asleep after a night shift, she and her mates would nick my car keys and rummage around in my car, looking for loose change so they could buy sweets at the shop. Ha, ha!

CHAPTER 23

SCHOOL FRIENDS

As soon as mobile phones came out, and were actually affordable enough to rent, I gave all my old school friends my number, and that was brilliant for everyone. I was the only one married at the time and all my school mates were single, so they would all be having wild nights out, and when I picked them up to take them home, I would hear all about their mad drunken exploits. All the one-night stands, married women, different types of threesomes, work colleagues, brewer's droop, wetting the bed, drunken falls and injuries, under-age mistakes, wedding receptions and bridesmaids, thrown out by bouncers, fights, crazy fancy dress, stag nights, Amsterdam red-light clubs, sickly ferry crossings, shagging fails, blowjobs and hangovers! I was just glad I was happily married.

About a month ago, I was staying at my son's house for a week, visiting friends and family. I got a message from my old school mates to say they were having a reunion the following evening. Well, what a night that was: six of us pissed as farts in Wetherspoons! I hadn't laughed so much in years. All the X-rated stories were re-told.

One of my favourites was the drunken ferry crossing. My best friend at school and best man at my wedding, Laurie 'H', used to be a European HGV lorry driver, and these drivers would get special treatment on the ferry crossings, including food and drink. My mate had brought along another school friend 'Croz' for the journey, and they were both enjoying the special food and drinks provided. When the sea started to get choppy, the school friend felt ill, so he went back to the cabin; but my best mate was used to the sea and finished off his food. On returning to the cabin, my best mate was met with a scene of absolute horror. The friend who was ill had not only puked up EVERYWHERE, but had blocked the toilet, so there was SHIT everywhere, AND he had managed to pull the waste pipe off the toilet, so a backlog of SHIT from other toilets was pouring into the cabin. I was crying with laughter at this story; so, so funny!

Whenever I went out drinking with my school friends, my missus was always a bit concerned, until one day that all changed for the good.

So, one summer's evening, I was out working, and my wife was indoors. Our teenage kids were playing outside and they got into a fight with a girl, who went home crying to her mum across the street. Two minutes later, her battleaxe beast of a mother came steaming across the road and started pounding on our big front window, threatening to beat my wife up. Leslie phoned me, but I was out of town, so I told her to phone 999. This is the conversation she had with the police controller. "Hello, this is an emergency. I've got a mad woman banging on my window threatening to beat me up. Can you send the police straight away?"

"Yes, madam. I've got your address here and I see you are Mrs Durtnall. Is your husband Adrian by any chance?"

"Yes, that's right, but what's that got to do with anything?"

"Well, you see, I went to school with Adrian and we were best friends. I am sending you three police cars right now; they will be there in three minutes, top priority."

So the police turned up and arrested the mad mum, and my school friend was the hero in my wife's eyes. So whenever I said I was going out with him for a drink, it was no problem at all.

CHAPTER 24

NEIGHBOURS

An incident that needed police attention was when my nasty next-door neighbour had a problem with us, and decided to come round and knock on our door. I opened the door and he started having a go at my wife, who was standing behind me. He was shouting and pointing past me and had obviously been drinking. He took a step inside our door, and as I pushed him out to shut the door, he punched me in the face, leaving a big red mark on my cheek. He ran off and quickly drove away in his car. I closed the door and phoned the police and said I wanted him done for assault, and that he was now drink-driving. When the police turned up, they could see the mark on my face and immediately put out an All-Points Bulletin on his car to find him. The police didn't locate him, but the next day I got a great phone call from the police station. My neighbour had only bloody gone into the station to try and report ME for assaulting him. They arrested him on the spot and put him in jail for the day. Ha, ha! I didn't press charges and so they released him. It all went very quiet after that incident.

So, after our nasty neighbours on one side decided to sell and move on, a lovely family moved in and we were good friends over the coming years. The neighbour situation on the other side was always changing, because it was a maisonette-style property that was run by the council as a half-way house for hard-up couples to stay for a while until they were housed properly. The worst tenants by far were a young couple with two young kids and a third on the way. The boyfriend would come home drunk from the pub every night and try to kick the front door in when she locked him out. Next, he would stand outside and shout up at the living room, swearing and cursing at her to let him in; and, of course, she would then start shouting back. At one point, he even put an old leather couch in the front garden and sat there in the summer with his usual cans of Stella during the day. All of us were in the front room trying to watch television, so we just turned the volume down because it was better than watching *EastEnders*. Of course, after a while we would be worried about our two cars on the driveway, especially my son's Focus ST, which was his pride and joy. I had to call the police numerous times, and even our opposite neighbours beat me to it.

This drama went on for about two years, which also involved her two kids being taken away from her, and the baby when it was born. After a big campaign by all the locals, they were finally evicted and the flat had to be totally gutted and refurbished.

Our good neighbours that moved into the house next door had a lovely driveway built to put their two nice cars on, and they were grateful to get them off the pavement next to the busy bend in the road. A few weeks later, a police car turned up outside my neighbours' house and started knocking on their door. I went out to talk to them, as neither of my neighbours' cars were there, so I assumed they had gone out and weren't at home. But, to my surprise, they both answered the door. I said, "Where are your cars?"

He said, "Last night, while we were asleep, two people broke into the house, stole our car keys and drove off with BOTH our cars."

Damn! That is some scary shit. The absolute nerve of some people. From that day onwards, we both put up security cameras, and kept all our car keys hidden indoors.

A lot used to happen near my house over the years for some reason.

One day, I came home for lunch, and as I was getting out of my car, the local special needs man, who had the mental age of about ten, walked right near me, closely followed by two eighteen-year-old tattooed girl thugs, who started punching him in the face and calling him a pervert. I went indoors, as I didn't want to get involved, but later I could see people asking for witnesses outside, so I said I would give the police a full statement and look at the mugshots. At the station, I gave my statement and then they showed me their mugshots of suspects. I only got to the third page and there she was. Boom! A hundred percent identification, no problem. I had to agree to attend court as a witness if necessary, which was a bit worrying, because they lived near to me.

Luckily, it was all sorted out of court, and I felt good for doing my duty.

Another incident outside my house occurred on my lunch break again. We lived at the start of a dangerous bend near a bus stop, so I would always park off the road near my driveway; but that particular day I had to park on the road. No sooner had I stepped indoors and put a sandwich in my mouth, when I heard a horrible screeching of brakes and crashing noises. As soon as I opened my front door, my mouth dropped open. Ooooh, SHIT! A bus coming up to the bend had swung out to drive round my car, but a fast car coming the other way round the bend had swerved to avoid the bus and crashed into five parked cars before it stopped. The bus had got wedged next to my car, trying to avoid a collision with the fast car. The police and an ambulance turned up, the road was closed off, and all witnesses questioned. All the damaged cars were taken away for assessments, which just left my car to be released from the scene. The bus was moved very carefully away from mine, and to my amazement the only damage to my car was a few scuffs and scratches, which I polished out with some T Cut. I thanked the bus driver for not writing my car off, and went back to work.

CHAPTER 25

BURGLARY

Holidays were always special times for my family and me. We would save up hard to have extra-special getaways. This time it was three wonderful weeks in Walt Disney World, Florida. We had friends of ours house-sitting for us, although they still had to work during the day, but this was very reassuring for us anyway. Three glorious weeks later, we returned home very tired and jet-lagged, only to be met at the door by our friends looking very upset. Our house had been burgled! It had been a daylight robbery while our friends were at work. They must have been disturbed halfway through, because all my computer and printer equipment was on the floor ready to go. They had forced their way in through the patio doors and taken jewellery and precious items. Thankfully, we were fully insured, and once the police had given us a crime number we put in our claim. The insurance company were brilliant and arranged everything for us. Unbelievably, we were given the sad news that on the day of the burglary, our house-sitters had discovered our kitten dead on the kitchen floor.

Some things you just can't replace, which was extremely upsetting for everyone. So, two weeks later, I got a phone call from our Blockbuster video store asking for their two videos back. They said if they didn't get them back we would be charged £500 for each video to replace them! I explained that it could not possibly have been us that took them out, because we were in Florida at the time. At this point I had a brainwave.

My Blockbuster card had been stolen in the burglary, so the cheeky bastards must have used it to take out the videos. I immediately phoned the police to tell them this, because I knew that Blockbuster use video surveillance on all the rentals at the counter, and they are Date and Time stamped. So, we all went down to Blockbuster with the police and reviewed the video footage to see who had rented out the videos. The person stepped up to the counter, we froze the frame, and I recognised him straight away. He knew when we were going on holiday, and must have planned the robbery himself. GOT YOU, ARSEHOLE! Straight away, the police rushed round to search his address, but found no incriminating evidence. They couldn't charge him with anything, but we all knew it was him.

CHAPTER 26

LIMO AND SKYDIVING

For my wife's fiftieth birthday, we secretly organised a big white limousine to pick up all seven of us and take us to the Grove Hotel near Watford for a really posh meal. On the day, all I said to her was that we were driving to a posh venue and should all dress up accordingly. The limo picked up my son first from his flat, and he rang me to tell me the limo was awesome. The limo pulled up outside our house. I turned round to my wife and put my car keys on the shelf and said, "Well, I won't be needing these now. Look out of the window."

I opened the door and she just screamed, "Oh my God! Wow!"

We all got in and started the party. Champagne on ice, party music and party poppers. We all made the most of the drinks and celebrated like mad. None of us had been in a limo before and we all thoroughly enjoyed the ride there and back. The hotel staff greeted us as the limo arrived, and escorted us to our fabulous sit-down buffet. My wife's cake arrived after the meal and just topped off a fabulous day. I was so glad that I had kept it all a secret for months beforehand, as it was such an amazing surprise on the day.

My family and I have always loved the different theme parks, adrenaline rides and roller-coasters, so when my son said he was going to do a skydive for charity, it was no surprise to us at all. He got all his required pledges and donations together, and set a date for the event. I drove him up to RAF Hinton in Oxfordshire, and it was a chilly but beautiful sunny morning in April. He had paid extra for his jump to be videoed, so they filmed him on the ground waiting to go, on the plane, and then the cameraman jumped out separately with him to film him face-to-face during the jump, landing before him so they could film his landing. Just amazing!

When he got the finished video back, it was all set to some great music soundtracks, and there was a separate disc with a hundred photos of the freefall that could be printed off and framed. The jumps were made from thirteen thousand feet, but from the ground you couldn't see anything, until the parachutes started opening just below the clouds. The landings were very soft and controlled, so you could walk away as soon as you landed. My son was very chilled out by the whole experience, but he did have a very cool instructor in the video.

Six months after my son's charity tandem skydive, having watched his video about fifty times, my daughter and my wife announced to me that they were BOTH going to do their skydives on the SAME day. This was a bit worrying for me, because my wife was fifty years old and disabled with a bad leg at the time, but crazy as she was, her mind was made up. In fact, she was more excited about it than our daughter. So a date was set, all pledges and donations made and videos booked. My Mum and Dad came along this time as they were semi-professional photographers, plus we were all immensely proud of both of them. It was a lovely sunny day and we knew they were in safe hands, because the joint owners were taking my wife and daughter up themselves. When I watched the video back of them on the plane, I got a lump in my throat, because my wife was so happy and waving all the time, knowing she was being filmed. As we stood on the ground and watched them land, I rushed over to check my wife was safe. But I needn't have worried, because when she got up off the ground, she said, "I absolutely loved it! I want to go back up and do it again!" Crazy woman!

One year later, and guess what? It's my turn. About two months before my skydive, I got lots of publicity by having an article written about my charity event in the local paper, and a few photos as well.

I can honestly say, to do a tandem skydive is one of the best adrenaline-filled, wonderful experiences you can ever have. When you fall out of the plane, you can only wave and smile at the cameraman opposite you because of all the wind and noise, and the fact that you have just done a full barrel roll, and are travelling at 120mph for thirty seconds of freefall! Then the worst bit is when the parachute opens and you surge upwards, and feel like you're going to be sick. When your heartbeat calms down, you can relax and take in the views as you gently float down for the super-soft landing. Once I had downed a whole bottle of water because of dehydration, I felt great again! Bring on the video! I printed off lots of photos of my dive and put them up in my car so everybody could see that I actually did do it.

CHAPTER 27

ADRENALINE JUNKIE

After my skydiving exploits, I became serious about needing adrenaline and adventure in my life. Well, it was a bit mundane driving my Ford Mondeo diesel slowly around town all day. So, every birthday and Christmas, I would always ask for Experience Gift Days Out, so I could get out of my comfort zone, so to speak. My first day out was a trip with my son to Everyman Racing in Leicester. A beautiful sunny day in June, with all the super cars lined up, gleaming in the sun: Ferraris, Lamborghinis, Porsches, Nissan GTRs, Aston Martins, Lotus, and the Ariel Atom for the Hot Laps. You had an instructor sitting next to you, giving you advice on how to hit the apex of the corner, when to brake and how to accelerate fast out of a corner. Very exciting in a car that is built for speed. After we had both driven a Ferrari and an Aston Martin, it was time for our Hot Laps in the Ariel Atom. Well, for starters, the driver was dressed like The Stig off *Top Gear*, and he drove like him as well. Jesus Christ, the acceleration was just insane! He went into the corners flat out, and just kept going the whole way round, overtaking everything in sight. These Atoms are just a framework, engine and four wheels, and your feet are right next to the front wheels and the track. I could see his speedo and at one point we under-took a Porsche at 120mph on a bend! You know that feeling you get when the ride finishes and you immediately want to go again? That's how I felt when we finished our three laps. If I'd had a spare £35,000 in my bank account that day, I would have bought one there and then. We had lots of photos taken for us around the track, including when we under-took the Porsche. Amazing day out!

Next trip out was a long day trip to drive a Caterham Seven sports car for six hours around the beautiful Cotswolds countryside, on a very hot July day. This time my wife was my passenger for the adventure, as she knew how much I loved these old-style sports cars. We were given our directions on a piece of paper, but this blew straight out of the car as soon as I accelerated off down a country lane. So Leslie became our navigator on my Google Maps. It was fun to start with, but after six hours driving a car that's like a sardine can, no power steering and no servo-assisted brakes, I was knackered; plus, being in an open-topped car, we had caught the sun badly!

Driving home in my car was a luxury compared to the Caterham.

Next trip was a helicopter flying experience with Flying Pigs, at Elstree Aerodrome. Another beautiful sunny day! This was actually my second time doing this experience, and was the better of the two, because I got to do more unaided flying this time. The pilot took me up to a comfortable height and speed, then showed me how to operate all the controls. The joystick was controlled by both of us, until you felt confident to do it by yourself. The controls were very sensitive, but once you had the feel, it was just a great experience. I flew over the M25 at a hundred knots, banked to the right and then straight, with the London skyline clearly far ahead. My pilot showed me the landing zone in the distance, and told me how to descend slowly with the lever. We were getting so close to the ground, I thought he was going to make me land the bloody thing – but at the last minute he took over the controls and spun it right round and started to hover. He said, "Right, now you can have a go at hovering."

Wow! I actually hovered for about thirty seconds and he was quite impressed. The whole flight was filmed from a fixed camera inside and set to *Top Gun* music.

Off to Silverstone next for a single-seater drive in a Formula Ford. We were all given racing overalls and crash helmets, and given instructions on the rules of racing. Those cars were like small Formula One cars, and we even lined up on a racing grid to start the event. The cars had just three gears on a lever next to your right leg, and no speedo. The track was amazing, and it was easy to overtake cars on the back straight, going flat out towards the bottom bend. Lap after lap you would get faster as you learned the racing line of the track and became more confident in your ability.

Photographers took great action shots around the track, and you chose the ones you wanted to be printed off at the end of the event.

I did outdoor and indoor go-karting with my son, which was always very competitive between us. I went to several Santa Pod drag racing events, which were extremely loud and the ground shook when they went past.

Next, I did a glider flight at Dunstable Downs They tow you up to a good height with an aeroplane and then release the glider from the tow-rope so you can soar upwards on the thermals and try to stay up as long as you can! The views were amazing, it flew quite fast, was very easy to fly with the basic controls and all you could hear was the wind rushing past on the extremely long wings. The really scary part was when my pilot started our descent and said that of course we have to get it right because we only get one chance!

We came in fast and flat and it was very bumpy, but as safe as you can make it on a large grass field! About a year later I was re-telling my gliding experience to my brother-in-law Tom, when he revealed to me that he actually part-owned a glider with his friend at Dunstable downs aerodrome and had once flown it non-stop all the way to the Isle of White, landed and returned all in one day! He explained that on the way back near London it got very cloudy and he lost his bearings, so luckily he made contact with one of his professional glider pilot friends on the radio and he was able to lead him all the way back to Dunstable! Wow! What an amazing achievement!

My most recent experience was a one-hour flight in a Microlight, in Cambridgeshire. A microlight looks like a big hang-glider with an engine on the back. The airstrip was just a very flat runway on smooth grass, and was a bit scary at full speed on take-off. Once in the air, everything is calm and smooth and quite relaxing. I was sitting squashed up behind the pilot, but all I had to do was put my hands up and hold on to the metal bar to control the glider, which was great fun. We went very low to start with over some houses, and you could see all the swimming pools in their gardens. It was very surreal and felt like we were spying on people.

Then we went really high and did a few dives, which made me feel a bit queasy. We then flew over to Grafham Water Sports Lake, and flew low and slow over the boats and canoes so we could wave to everybody as we passed over them. My pilot was very chatty and knowledgeable, and was constantly pointing out interesting sights as we flew over them. The landing was easy and straightforward; even I could have attempted it! I thoroughly enjoyed myself doing some flying on this trip and would definitely do it again.

CHAPTER 28

DIESEL NIGHTMARE

In 2002, I ended up talking live on a BBC Radio consumer affairs programme about a serious issue I had with my local Ford main dealer.

So, about three weeks before this, I was on my school run in my Mk2 diesel Mondeo, which was only eighteen months old and had about eighteen thousand miles on the clock. The car started to splutter and the acceleration was poor, so when I got home I changed the fuel filter, and that seemed to cure the problem for a few days. Then, whilst driving around town, the car just conked out and wouldn't start again. I called the AA, but they couldn't get it going either, so they towed me up to the Ford main dealer, which was, thankfully, only five minutes' walk from my house. The next day I phoned the garage and I was told that they would start investigating the problem. Five days later: "Hello, Mr Durtnall, we've found the fault on your engine. Are you sitting down?

"Well, the fault is called Fuel Contamination, and this means the wrong type of fuel has been put in the car and caused the rubber seals on the fuel pump to break up, dissolve, and contaminate the whole fuel system. So you need a complete new fuel system, which is going to cost £2000 to complete. We have a test tube of the contaminated fuel that was analysed by BP."

What a load of BOLLOCKS! I went fucking mental down the phone at them! Luckily for me, I kept all my diesel receipts, and I had proof that I had filled up at the same garage seven days on the trot before my car broke down, and told them to double-check the diesel quality at their pumps. The result of their tests was that their fuel was perfect. So, after confronting the main dealer with MY diesel receipts and having had a blazing row with them and threatening to go to the papers and sue their arses, they backed down with the original quote, but I still had to pay £1200. In all, I was off the road for twelve days, which was bloody annoying as well. So, with my blood still boiling, I arranged to go on the radio show and air my frustrations. Although I was not allowed to name the dealership in question, it felt good to talk with some experts and warn other drivers of this possible problem with that diesel car. I found out about a year later from a mechanic friend of mine that Ford had lots of problems with those fuel pumps and later changed their suppliers. So I knew then that I was in the right the whole time.

On another occasion at my local Ford main dealer, I booked my car in because it was smoking badly when accelerating. I was told that it needed a new turbo, new injectors and a new EGR (exhaust gas recirculation) valve. The quote for all this was £3000! I politely told them where to shove their quote and drove up to my mechanic's house.

He laughed and told me about the not-so-legal way of getting around the problem. He ordered an EGR blanking plate off the internet, and put a large dose of injector cleaner in the fuel tank to clear the injectors. Two days later, with the blanking plate fitted, I gave it a good thrashing down the bypass. All the black, smokey shit came out of the exhaust and then cleared itself. Job done for the grand total of £20! The only down side to this fix was that the engine management light would keep coming on, so at MoT time I had to use a portable coding machine to clear this fault light just before the MoT to get it through the emissions test.

That Mondeo went on to clock up three hundred and ten thousand miles by the time I had finished with it. I was trying to sell it privately because my Dad had very kindly bought me a new car, as I couldn't get finance any more. It was in very good condition, but nobody wanted it; so, as usual, the gypsies came knocking and said they would buy it, but only because they wanted the bonnet and wings to repair their car. OK! No problem with that. Sold!

CHAPTER 29

MONUMENTAL MOVE

Over the last few years of my long taxi career my wife's health and mobility had deteriorated so much that she now needed a wheelchair and indoor scooter to get around. My daughter and friends helped with her care while I was at work, but with me working long hours, it was no life for her at home like that, so we came up with a big life-changing plan. We planned to sell our house, pay off the mortgage, buy a bungalow outright somewhere, then I would retire and be her full-time carer. So, in September 2016, the house went on the market and we had plenty of viewings. Our search for a bungalow took months and eventually my wife suggested living by the sea, and Lowestoft was in our price range. At the end of January 2017, we had a firm offer on our house by first-time buyers, so we lined up five bungalow viewings in Lowestoft for the Monday. I had an alert set up on Rightmove so that anything new on the market would show up straight away. The Sunday night before we travelled down, I was alerted to a bungalow new to the market that day, so Monday morning, before we left, I rang the estate agent to arrange a viewing for later that day.

The original five viewings didn't go that well, because they needed too much work doing to them and our budget didn't stretch that far, so we were very disappointed by then. The final viewing was the last-minute one, so we were the first to view it. Well, we walked in and we loved it straight away! It was like a palace compared to all the others, and nothing needed doing to it. The owner was there to show us around, and we agreed the price on the spot, each of us doing the necessary phone calls to make the deal secure. Back at home after a very long day out, we all celebrated and arranged the moving date.

My next move was to arrange the sale of my Hackney Taxi plate. Although you couldn't officially sell the plate, unofficially they were like gold dust to certain drivers who were desperate to get hold of these saloon-only-type plates, so were willing to pay big cash-in-hand for them. I got £5500 for mine, and just transferred the plate into his name. Result!

Moving day arrived, but the day before everything had been packed into a huge articulated lorry and another smaller van. Friday morning, the lorries set off for Lowestoft and we had to wait until midday to hand over the keys. Now it was a three-hour drive to Lowestoft, and solicitors don't usually complete house sales until about three thirty p.m., so it was a very nervous drive to our new home, waiting for the phone call from the solicitors to say it had completed. On the way down, we got a phone call from the removal men to say they had access to our new garden and were starting to unload most of our stuff there, as it was thirty degrees and we could open the garage and house when we got the keys.

Just as we arrived in Lowestoft, we got the exciting news from the solicitor that everything had completed and we could go and pick up the keys from the estate agents in the town centre. Oh, the relief! We opened up the empty garage and house, but all our boxes (a hundred!) filled the garage to the very brim as well as the bungalow extension. Downsizing is hard work!

Two weeks after moving Leslie and I were just out exploring our new high street when I looked up and couldn't believe my eyes! Walking towards us was my best regular and friend, Stan and his grown-up daughter! "Bloody hell, what are you doing here Stan, are you on holiday?"

"No I moved here last year to sell holiday rentals with my friend and now we are going to open our own estate agents called Langwrights! Over the next few years they built up a good business together and it was great to have my mate close by to socialise with!

We made several visits back to Hemel to visit family, friends and all the Asda drivers over the years, but of course when the COVID lock-downs and furlough started it had a massive impact on the taxi industry and a lot of the drivers were really struggling to survive. I was so lucky that I got out of Taxiing when I did because I wouldn't have been able to pay the mortgage during that very worrying time!

The next two and a half years were just amazing, being together every day and exploring all the lovely beaches, our local marina and the surrounding countryside. I transformed the back garden with decking, slabs and artificial grass to make it all independently wheelchair-friendly, and the front garden ramped as well, with lovely driveway blocks and more artificial grass. Indoors got completely redecorated and furnished as well.

Then, at the end of October 2019, Leslie found a lump and was diagnosed with Triple Negative breast cancer. We were devastated. Aimee was due to visit us a week later and it was the hardest thing we had ever done to break the tragic news of Leslie's diagnosis! Because of her already long-term illness of Scleroderma, they did not advise radio- or chemotherapy, which pretty well meant that she was now going to go downhill fast. Thankfully, she was made comfortable at home with us during the COVID pandemic. I heard so many horror stories of loved ones stuck in hospitals and NO relatives being allowed in to see them. Our son came to stay, and for Leslie's last six weeks we were all together at home to make her comfortable and take her mind off things by playing simple games like cards, chess, and Pop-up Pirates. The palliative care team from the hospital were brilliant and made sure that our extension was kitted out with everything we needed, from a proper hospital bed to all medicines and other products.

We took it in shifts to attend to anything Leslie needed, so we could all get some sleep. The final days were very stressful and emotional, until Leslie passed away peacefully on 5th July 2020.

The funeral was right in the middle of the pandemic but fortunately we were still allowed thirty guests, as the graveside service was being held outside with a bluetooth speaker for the music. We had all contributed to a beautiful eulogy which was read aloud by the funeral director at our request and Leslie was laid to rest at our local natural burial park, in a beautiful wicker basket coffin with woven flowers all over. Everyone came back for the wake at the bungalow afterwards and I was just so amazed and overwhelmed at listening to all of Aimee and Russell's friends reminiscing about growing up together and all the wonderful memories of Leslie. Our house was always full of Aimee and Russell's friends because Leslie and I were there during the day and it was like a social club for them with food, snacks and drinks laid on by Leslie, music and wild kids' parties with water fights and tree houses to play on! All these friends who are now in their thirties were so thankful to Leslie for their brilliant childhood memories and who now make sure that their children do exactly the same as they did, by having as much fun as possible!

CHAPTER 30

MEDIUMS

A couple of months after the funeral, my daughter and I decided we should try going to an outdoor medium event being held at a local hotel. Now Leslie and I were true believers in the spirit world, and I felt sure that she would try to contact us in some way. Well, she did. Several times, in fact!

I was all ready to go to the medium event and was sitting in our extension, waiting for my daughter to get ready, and just had my head down, browsing on my phone. I started to hear a ticking noise, and I looked up at the cuckoo clock. Now, this clock hadn't worked for about two years because it became too annoying, so we stopped the pendulum on it to keep it quiet.

All the doors and windows were closed, ready for us to leave, so there was no wind blowing through. The pendulum on the clock just started swinging and ticking on its own for about fifteen seconds and stopped – and never did it again. Freaky!

So we got to the hotel and everybody was sitting in their own private groups outside under the canopies. The medium was just brilliant, and we all listened sadly as he spoke to each group about their loved ones, and the emotional and comforting messages they wanted to pass on to them. The medium came to us last, and said straight away, "You've lost your wife very recently, Mum to your daughter sitting next to you. She's a very strong spirit and she truly believed in the afterlife. She was also very pissed off about having to leave you both, but heaven is better than she thought it was going to be."

Now these messages were very emotional and spot on for us, because he had just described her to a tee. We just cried tears of joy, because we knew it was her speaking through him, and it gave us so much comfort to know she was in a good place.

My daughter and I have had a very strong belief in the spirit world after seeing a famous medium with Leslie, in Watford many years ago, and being shocked to the core by what she told us.

When Leslie was a teenager, she lost her mum to multiple sclerosis, and if that wasn't bad enough, her nasty step-dad had her mum buried at a secret location in another town, far away. After we were married and living in our house, Leslie would always see a shadowy figure going up the stairs, and was constantly annoyed at not being able to go to her mother's grave. So when somebody suggested this famous medium, we decided to give her a try. We all went to her house, except for our son, who was seventeen at the time, and had only passed his driving test a few months before, and was working that day. We all sat in her bedroom and listened intently to her rambling on about all sorts of things, which all made sense to us, and we all nodded and smiled in acknowledgement. Then she said, "You are worried about your son's fast driving! Your daughter was very hard work as a teenager and was always getting into trouble with the police!"

How did she know about our son, who wasn't even there? Then a real strange statement. "Leslie, your Mum and real Dad are standing behind you and she is telling you not to worry now as HER GRAVE HAS NOW BEEN FOUND."

Well, we both looked at each other and then both said to the medium, "No, that can't be right because we've tried looking and found no trace of it."

We were very pleased with the medium experience, but obviously a bit puzzled with her revelation. Two months later, we got a phone call from Leslie's brother, asking us to come over to their house for an important chat. As soon as we sat down, they said that they had a confession to make. SIX MONTHS ago they had found something and had held off from telling Leslie, to avoid upsetting her. They had been privately searching for the grave and had FOUND IT SIX MONTHS AGO. We were both flabbergasted, because the medium had been right! The grave had been found FOUR MONTHS before we went to the medium. WOW! We made several visits to pay our respects, and Leslie could finally put this horrible event behind her. Also, Leslie never saw the shadowy figure on the stairs any more.

Over the next year we had a few private sessions with our local medium, and Leslie came through strongly every time, and was now always with her mum! More strange and mind-blowing events also happened in our house later on. My daughter had a very close friend who lived in Hemel Hempstead and came all the way here for the funeral, to comfort her on the day. They would have long heart-to-heart chats on the phone afterwards and she was a great comfort to my daughter. One evening, whilst having one of these chats, we heard a great big crash in the kitchen. I got up to investigate and in the middle of the kitchen floor were two big cooking utensils that had been in a large ceramic jar on the top shelf. Freaky! One week later, during a phone chat with the same friend again, this time a big white tree ornament on the dresser just toppled over sideways all on its own right in front of us. Freaky! One month later, my daughter got a very excited phone call from this special friend again. "I've just been to my regular psychic meeting here in Hemel and your Mum came through to speak to me, to thank me for being a good friend and coming to the funeral. She also mentioned a ring as well."

Well, we were just gobsmacked. Leslie obviously had this connection with my daughter's best friend, who she had never actually known in her lifetime. The ring mentioned was also startling, because it had been mentioned in ALL of our private readings as well.

So, after seeing our favourite medium, alone and with my daughter several times, one message that was coming through loud and clear was that Leslie was going to send me a lovely, special woman for me to meet and be good companions with. She would not be local to me, but not too far away. It was clearly a message from Leslie, telling me it was OK to find someone else and move on with my life. All our medium sessions had been amazing, with so many comforting messages, which were great therapy for us both, and also PROOF that it really was Leslie we were communicating with.

CHAPTER 31

DATING

So, two years after Leslie's passing, my son and I went on holiday to Tenerife to recharge our batteries at a great five-star resort, where we enjoyed all the hot sunshine, local restaurants and nightlife. On my return, I was obviously still in holiday mood and felt great about myself, so I did what everybody else does now and went on the Facebook dating site. Well, it was a bit of a learning curve for me, and I had to keep adjusting my profile after reading everyone else's. A week went by and nobody took my fancy, or I didn't get any matches. There was one woman who was the very first suggestion on my page, because we had one Facebook friend in common and whom I instantly found attractive from her photos, and so I 'liked' her straight away. I had no response from her, so I just carried on with my searching.

About five days after me 'liking' this woman, I was driving up to Northampton for a big family summer party for a couple of days, when I got a 'ping' on my phone to say I had a match with this woman I had fancied at the very beginning! I was so excited that I had to pull into the next services to message her back. She instantly explained that the delay in 'liking' me back was because she had been at the Latitude Festival for four days solid, and had been catching up on her sleep. We arranged a meet-up at a café near her home, as I would be passing there on my way back two days later. I was so chuffed and excited on my drive up to the summer family party, and blurted it out straight away when I arrived. All my family were so pleased for me and wished me luck.

Having just driven from my family party, I was dressed in white shorts, trainers, a tropical blue shirt and cool mirrored sunglasses! As I now like to call her, my first impression of her was 'hippy chick, festival girl' style. We soon found out that we had a lot in common, including the fact that we had both grown up in the same town. We had the same sense of humour and were both chilled and relaxed about everything. She worked as a carer, so after an hour she had to rush off to her next client, but we had a nice hug and set up on Facebook Messenger.

Our next date was great. She drove to my town and we had a meal next to my local beautiful marina and park, enjoyed the swans and birds and chatted about everything. I then took her for a scenic drive around our local town highlights in my Mercedes, which she loved. I must admit that romance wasn't on the cards for her, although we did get along very well together.

Going on dates was difficult to arrange because of her work commitments, and having only two weekends off a month. Fortunately, I am a very patient man, and eventually an opportunity came up where she was going to drop her son off in Norwich and I could meet her there for a meal in the evening.

It was a beautiful summer's Saturday evening, and we both parked up and took a leisurely stroll through the restaurant areas. She was my guide, because it was my first night out in Norwich, and everywhere was rammed. Each place we tried to get into was fully booked or an hour's wait. We had such a laugh, because every time we were waiting at the entrances, she would grab a handful of chocolate mints when they weren't looking, like a couple of schoolkids. Eventually, we had to move our cars because of the time restrictions, so she drove around the town looking for another place to eat, and I followed on some sort of wild-goose chase until we had driven around the town about three times. We eventually parked up, walked down some stairs and then, bam! There in front of us was this great Thai restaurant. The food was amazing, and both of us had a couple of beers each. We had a great time and talked non-stop about our lives, and laughed and joked a lot after a few drinks. I asked for the bill and, as usual, we split it between us. I looked at the bill and laughed my head off, because my beer had been normal and hers was NON-ALCOHOLIC!

What made it even worse was that because of a previous medical problem, she hadn't been allowed to drink ALL YEAR. Until now. She just put her head in her hands and said, "I don't bloody believe it, ha, ha!"

We hugged, drove our separate ways home, and had a good laugh messaging each other. The next day, I went for my usual one-hour swimming session, and was on such a high from a great night out that I swam sixty-six lengths! Swimming has been brilliant for me in so many ways, and I try to go at least five times a week for an hour each time.

A few months later my companion changed her job which meant she could have every weekend off and I thought we could now plan ahead for some fun social events, but unfortunately she had other ideas. So one evening she told me that I should go on a blind date with her best friend, who was also a widow and we had a lot of things in common! I soon got the hint and messaged her friend for a date the next day.

The blind date went very well and we talked non-stop for four hours about our lives and adventures! Three more dates quickly followed and we soon realised that we had strong feelings for each other. As our relationship blossomed we began planning several festivals, concerts, weekend breaks, small holidays and big holidays! A medium had foretold of our meeting two and a half years beforehand and we now realised how fortunate we were to have found each other after the loss of both our long-term partners!

CHAPTER 32

BONDING AND ENJOYING LIFE AGAIN

My daughter and I have a close relationship now, and try to do a lot of new experiences together. Now that we live near the beach, one thing she has always wanted to do was horse riding on the beach. So, one lovely sunny October day, we booked up at our local stables, and got all saddled up with about six other riders. I must say I felt quite safe and relaxed on my horse, even though it was my first time. Slowly trotting along the sand next to the sea was just brilliant, and will definitely be repeated again some time. The stable girls took some great photos of us together, which have now been framed.

Other fun days out have been had on my big twelve-foot dinghy that we use on our local marina. We take our dog Cookie with us and she wears her bright yellow life jacket. We just take a picnic with us and paddle slowly around, looking at all the other boats and the waterfront houses. We sail past and wave at the residents sitting in their gardens, and they wave back. When we're finished, the boat just deflates, and everything fits into my boot for our drive home.

Now I was back on the social scene, my best friend here and his girlfriend invited me to go on a Soul River Boat Cruise, going up the Broads from our local marina. It was a beautiful July evening, and after pre-drinks at the wine bar, we boarded the boat. The disco was in full swing, with two DJs and a busy bar. The boat had an open-top level for sightseeing, as well as having open views from the main dancing level.

We made lots of new friends on the trip and the music was just brilliant. It was such a smooth trip, you forgot you were on the water and just danced like mad. Three hours later and we docked back at the marina. Of course, we were all still buzzing, and just headed over to the local bars. Being a Saturday night, there was a queue to get in the most popular bar, so about eight of us went to the next bar and found it to be empty. BUT in the function room there was a disco floor with a DJ blaring out loud music. We all stood at the door to the function room and realised it was a wedding reception. Then the bride came over to us and said we were welcome to come in as no one was using the dance floor, and the DJ was going on till one a.m. RESULT! Flash mob ready to party. We couldn't believe our luck. Spur of the moment wedding gatecrashers!

PARTY, PARTY! What a great night!

My new adventures on the journey we all call LIFE will continue at a slower pace now. This book has been a roller-coaster of emotions for me, from age twenty-one to fifty-nine, and every word has been TRUE! As they say, "Truth is stranger than fiction, and you couldn't make it up!"

For all of those twenty-nine years of taxi driving, everyone who listened to my stories as I was ferrying them around would always tell me, "You should write a book when you retire!"

So now I have, and I really hope you enjoyed reading it as much as I enjoyed living and writing it. For me, as someone going through the grieving process, writing this book has been a very therapeutic and healing experience; and, of course, all the mediums that have bought my daughter and I such comforting messages and proof that Leslie is still with us in spirit! God bless her!